Aquitaine: A Traveller's Tales

Wickham Flower

AQUITAIN

AQUITAINE

A TRAVELLER'S TALES

BY

WICKHAM FLOWER, F.S.A.

WITH ILLUSTRATIONS
BY
JOSEPH PENNELL

Reproduced by the Art Reproduction Company

LONDON
CHAPMAN AND HALL, LIMITED
HENRIETTA STREET, COVENT GARDEN, W.C.
1897

LONDON :

PRINTED BY WILLIAM CLOWES AND SONS, LIMITED,
STAMFORD STREET AND CHARING CROSS.

PREFACE.

In the west of France, about midway between Paris and Bordeaux, stands, on a steep hill in the midst of a plain, the City of Poitiers, capital of the ancient country of Aquitaine, a country bounded for its whole distance on the west by the Aquitanian or Western sea, now known as the Bay of Biscay: on the north by the River Loire: on the south by the mountains of the Pyrenees, except that the little kingdom of Navarre filled the south-west corner of the country immediately south of Bayonne: and on the east by a line drawn from near Blois to Toulouse, and thence to the mountains, taking in the projecting part of the province of Auvergne that lies to the east of the line.

The country was known in ancient times as the Gaul of Aquitaine, to distinguish it from the more

northern countries of Celtic Gaul and Belgic Gaul.
It is, as its name denotes, "a land of many waters"
—fountains, rivers and streams. These and its rich
soil, fine climate, and the great forests and famous
vineyards of Gascony, made the country in times
of old what it is still—the richest and most
prosperous part of France.

In modern times the name of the country and
the ancient land-marks have been altered: Poitiers is
now in the department of the Vienne, Bordeaux in
that of the Gironde, Toulouse in the Haute Garonne,
Albi in the department of the Tarn, Perigeux in that
of the Dordogne ; but as that part of its history that
is told of in this book is of the times when the
country was known only as Aquitaine, that name
alone will be referred to, and so it will be easier
to follow the stories on the old maps.

To many travellers—probably to most—the city
of Poitiers is a place that, in comparison with other
cities of far less interest, is little visited and little
known. Yet it is not too much to say of it that there

is no city of France of greater interest, none possessed of more historical importance, than this, the capital of the once great country of Aquitaine.

From the days when in the first century the Emperor Claudius passed through the country after he had been raised by the Roman soldiers to supreme power, upon the murder of Caligula, and, according to an old tradition, on his way through France to invade Britain and suppress a revolt of the Britons against the Roman rule, he created a " new king " in Aquitaine—" crea ung aultre Roy en Aquitaine qui est aultrement appellé Procureur "—and took this king and a certain number of the nobles and inhabitants of Poitiers, and the people of Poitou—" gens hardiz et de hault couraige "—to assist in the suppression of the rebellion—for which service the Emperor allowed the people to rebuild their city on its present site—till that day on which Henry Plantagenet, King Henry II. of England, Count of Poitiers, passed to his rest in his favourite castle of Chinon, on the river Vienne, in the month of May, 1189

—the history of Poitiers has been one of surpassing and continuous interest. But it must be read—and can only be read rightly—by the light of the old books.

By such books—to name but some of them— as the "Itinerarium of Antoninus," begun in the time of Julius Cæsar and revised and completed in the time of Marcus Aurelius; the "History of Gregory of Tours"; the history known as the "Patrologiœ Cursus Completus" of Migne; the works of Saint Fortunatus; the lives of the saints in the "Acta Sanctorum," the great work of the Bollandists; Vaissette's History of Languedoc; L'Art de Verifier les Dates des Faits Historiques; the "Chronicles of Matthew Paris, Ordericus Vitalis and William of Malmesbury"; the "Chronicles of France," by Belleforest; "Les Temps Mérovingeans," by Thierry; Sismondi's "Litterature du Midi de l'Europe"; the Anglo-Norman romance—"Le Roman de Rou"; the romance of Master Wace of "the Isle of Jersey in the Western Sea"; the "Eulogium of the

Monk of Malmesbury"; the "Rhymed Chronicle
of Chandos Herald"; and the "Chronicle of Geoffrey
Le Baker, of Swynebroke"; the "Chronicles
of Froissart"; the "Annals of Aquitaine, and the
sayings and doings of the Kings of France and
England, and of the Countries of Naples and
Milan," published at about the beginning of the
sixteenth century by Master Jehan Bouchet, a citizen
of Poitiers, Procureur of the King; the "History
of King Clotaire and his very illustrious wife
Madame Sainte Radegonde," published in 1517 by
Bouchet; the "Golden Legend, or Lives of the
Saints," a beautiful edition of which was published a
few years ago by Mr. W. Morris; "Champollion's
documents inédits sur l'histoire de France"; "Eyton's
Itinerary of the reign of Henry II."; "M. Belisaire
Ledain's Histoire sommaire de Poitiers" (the last
two being comparatively modern books); and some
biographies of persons spoken of in the following
stories, among the best of them being Mr. Cotter
Morrison's "Life of Saint Bernard," and that most

b

charming and delightful contemporary sixth century story of the " Life of Sainte Radegonde," by her friend and companion, the nun Baudonovie.

Reference to a few of the great events that happened in the first .twelve hundred years of the Christian era in the country and in the city will give a general idea of the importance of the history of Aquitaine.

In the first century there is the story—the old tradition that is much treasured in Poitiers—of the invasion of Britain by the Romans, in alliance with the people of Poitiers, and the subsequent building of the existing city. The evangelisation of Aquitaine by Saint Martial, and the life of the Saint —a frequent visitor to Poitiers, and a citizen of Limoges, whose story is full of exciting and picturesque incidents. In the second century came the building of the vast Roman amphitheatre at Poitiers —in the time of the Emperor Marcus Aurelius—a building that would hold twenty-two thousand spectators ; and the magnificent aqueducts, and the Palais

Galienne. These two centuries and the earlier part of the third century were to the citizens times of peace and great prosperity under the Roman protection and rule.

In the third century came the invasion of the country by the barbarian Germans—the Franks and the Vandals, who twice sacked Poitiers with great destruction to the country and the town.

The fourth century was a period of great importance in the history of the city, for at that time lived the Emperor Constantine, the builder of Constantinople, whose mother Helaine was the daughter of an English innkeeper. It was Constantine who first sanctioned the building of Christian churches in the city. In his time lived Saint Hilary, a citizen of Poitiers and the most famous clerk in Gaul, and that famous Saint and Father of the Christian church, who was his disciple—Saint Martin of Tours. Saint Athanasius and Saint Nicholas of Myra were, in a way, connected by their stories with the city. The Greek priest Heliodorus taught Saint Hilary Greek in his own university of Poitiers. Here also came Ausonius, the Roman poet of Bordeaux.

In the fifth century Poitiers and the country of Aquitaine were given by the Emperor Honorius to the Visigoths, who were Arians. And the Arian heresy prevailed in the country, and the Kings of the Visigoths lived in Poitiers for nearly a hundred years.

In the sixth century Clovis, King of the Franks, conquered the Visigoths, and drove their King Alaric out of the country. Then followed the rule of the Merovingean Kings—the descendants of Clovis—in Aquitaine: and this was one of the most interesting periods in the history of the city, as it takes in the lives of Sainte Radegonde and Saint Fortunatus, and something of the story of the Emperor Justin II., successor to Justinian, as well. To this period also belongs the sad and most pathetic story of Galsuinthe, the beautiful daughter of Athanagilde, the King of the Visigoths, who came to Poitiers from Toledo to become the wife of Chilpéric, King of Soissons, and after a short reign was strangled by her husband's order, and in his presence, by the hands of a slave.

During the whole of the seventh century Aquitaine and the city of Poitiers suffered severely through the constant civil wars of the Merovingean kings, the descendants of Clovis, who ruled the country, till at last with the eighth century there grew up a new power in the country—that of Pepin d'Heristal, Mayor of the Palace, and his more famous son, Charles Martel—he who while ruling the people with supreme power always disdained to take upon himself the title of King.

Whilst speaking of Sainte Radegonde, the great rebellion of the nuns of the Abbey of Sainte Croix should be mentioned, when, shortly after the Queen's death, two of the nuns of the blood royal—Chrodielde, daughter of Caribert, King of Paris, and Basine, daughter of Chilpéric, King of Neustria—fought with mercenary troops and bandits, headed by Childéric the Saxon, against the Abbess Leubovère. They, with fifty of their companions, in consequence of a quarrel with the Abbess, whom they wished to depose and to elect Chrodielde in her place, absconded to Gontran, the King of Burgundy, and, encouraged by him, returned to the city with an armed force of men of evil character, bandits and homicides, and entrenched themselves in the enceinte of the church of Saint Hilary. A series of terrible fights occurred in the streets of Poitiers between the soldiers of the Abbess and those of the nuns, which ended finally, after great loss of life, in the submission of the nuns.

The eighth century was a great period in the history of the country and the city, for it takes in the capture of the city and the complete rout of the Saracens by Charles Martel, and the succession of his son, Pepin the Little—by whom the country was brought entirely under the dominion of the French kings—who was succeeded by his son the Emperor Charlemagne. The famous Alcuin, the friend and protégé of Charlemagne, was a frequent visitor to the city, and is said to have filled the church of Saint Hilary and its chapels with his epitaphs and poems.

In the ninth century Louis le Debonnaire, the son of Charlemagne, ruled in Aquitaine and constantly lived in Poitiers. Three times in this century was the country invaded and the city attacked, and partly burnt by the Norman pirates. Towards the end of the century the famous Benedictine Abbey of Cluny was founded and endowed by Guillaume le Pieux, Count of Poitiers and Duke of Aquitaine.

In the tenth century, Ebles, Duke of Aquitaine, married Adèle, daughter of Edward the Old, King of the Anglo-Saxons. Parts of the present church of Saint Hilary were built by the Duchess, who died and was buried in her own monastery of La Trinité in Poitiers.

In the eleventh century William of Poitiers, the historian and chaplain of William the Conqueror, was a citizen of Poitiers. He, according to a custom of his time, is known only by the name of the city that gave him education—William of Poitiers.

Thus by a like custom were known Dudo of Saint Quentin, William of Jumieges, William of Malmesbury, William of Newbury, Roger of Wendover, the Abbot of Peterboro', Matthew Paris, and many more.

And throughout the tenth, eleventh, and twelfth centuries there reigned in Poitiers a long and illustrious line of Dukes of Aquitaine and Counts of Poitiers, of wealth, position, and power, as great as, often greater than, that of the kings of France, ending only in the year 1137 with the death of Duke William, who was the father of our Queen Eleanor, in whose right the duchy passed on her marriage with King Henry II., in the year 1152, to the English crown.

Such is but a slight outline of some of the many great historical events that mark the history of the country of Aquitaine, and the city of Poitiers for the first twelve hundred years of its existence. And such are the names of some of the most famous of its citizens; and I have mentioned some of the books —the ancient books—out of which alone the story can be told. It can, I think, hardly be doubted that for the true and perfect appreciation of any city or any country, a knowledge of its history is essential. It is essential that, by that knowledge, one should be able to people the air, as it were, with thoughts and fancies of the past, and with actual visions of the great events that have occurred in it, and of the great and famous people who have lived and moved and had their being there in times gone by. And probably there is no city of which this may be said more truly than of Poitiers, where, in comparatively so small a compass, so many events of the greatest historical importance and interest have occurred.

The very air of the place is full to overflowing of visions of the past. " Des mirages d'histoire flottent partout dans l'air de Poitiers," says a French historian —the mists and shadows of history fill the very air. Therefore, let everyone who goes to Poitiers take with him some acquaintance with its story, and with the many picturesque and interesting legends and traditions of the country of which that story

is so largely composed. In a fine passage in the
"Defence of Poesy," Sir Philip Sidney reminds
us of the debt we owe to various poets for the
beauty they have added to the beauty of the
country, thus :—" Nature," says he, " Nature never
set forth the earth in so rich tapestry as diverse
poets have done, neither with so pleasant rivers,
fruitful trees, sweet-smelling flowers, nor whatsoever
else may make the too much loved earth more
lovely. Her world is brazen — the poets only
deliver a golden."

And as one calls to mind a few among many of
the English poets who have described to us in
exquisite and enchanting terms the beauties of the
country, commencing with Chaucer in the last half
of the fourteenth century, and with him Piers Plowman and Gower, followed in the fifteenth century
by Dunbar and Gawain Douglas,—by Spenser and
Shakespeare in the sixteenth,—Ben Jonson, Herrick,
and Milton in the seventeenth,—Gray and Burns in
the eighteenth—and in the century still unfinished

Sir Walter Scott, Leigh Hunt, Shelley, Keats, Tennyson, William Morris, and Browning—one recognises how true that saying of Sir Philip Sidney's is. How true it is that Nature hath not set forth the world in so rich a tapestry as diverse poets have done.

And can it be doubted that we owe at least as great a debt to the historians of the middle ages, for they have set the story of the world before us, and by the light of it we look upon the ancient towns and cities and the countries that surround them with an infinitely greater interest than they would otherwise possess.

If it be true that the poets have clothed the world with beauty that, but for them, would be wanting to it, just as true it is that the historians have imparted to it an interest and a picturesqueness that but for them would be unknown. So should the beautiful country be always looked at by the light of poetry and by the light of history, and, above all, the most ancient history, for that is always the best.

In the following chapters are set forth some

of the stories of the city of Poitiers and the country of Aquitaine that, in the autumn of 1896, I (a traveller in the country) composed and put together, whilst on a visit to Poitiers, and sent to England as letters to a friend, by whose assistance and advice they were afterwards revised and amplified, and are now published in the present form. And it is to be hoped that by other hands, some other day, this work may be continued, and that thus that complete knowledge of the country—that now, to a great extent, is only obtainable by a laborious examination of books not easily accessible—may, in days to come, be made easy of acquirement by travellers who desire to visit Poitiers and the rich, beautiful, and interesting country that lies around it —the country of Aquitaine.

OLD SWAN HOUSE, CHELSEA EMBANKMENT.
October, 1897.

CONTENTS.

LIST OF ILLUSTRATIONS.

ERRATUM.

Page 116 (last line but two) *for* eighteenth or nineteenth century *read*
eighth or ninth century.

Tales of the three great battles that were fought in times of old around the ancient city of Poitiers. And first, of the battle that was fought by Clovis, King of the Franks, against the Visigoths, under Alaric, King of Aquitaine, A.D. 507.

Tales of the three great battles that were fought in times of old around the ancient city of Poitiers. And first, of the battle that was fought by Clovis, King of the Franks, against the Visigoths, under Alaric, King of Aquitaine, A.D. 507.

THE stories of these battles were compiled during a summer holiday in 1896,

" In a somer seson, when softe was the sonne

.   .   .   . I

Went wyde in this world, wondres to here."

partly from well-ascertained facts of history, and partly from the "traditions, legends, tales and songs," and the romances of the country of Aquitaine —they are the tales of a traveller, and so far as their authenticity may be considered in any respect doubtful, that indulgence is claimed for them that since the days of the dream of Piers Plowman has always been willingly accorded to stories of the kind.

" Pilgrims and Palmers
　Plighten them together
　For to seek Saint James
　And the Saints at Rome.
　They went forth on their way
　With many wise tales,
　And had leave to lyen
　All their life after."

It will, of course, be recognised that in writing of times as old as those of King Clovis and Charles Martel, one has to depend rather upon the ancient traditions—and the beliefs of the people of the country—than upon any carefully written record of the events of the times, and if those traditions and that belief are not always in agreement with the actual facts of history as we know them now, they undoubtedly possess an extraordinary picturesqueness, an interest, and a charm that one could ill afford to lose. The world would indeed be the poorer if from the pages of its history were excluded all that is considered to be of doubtful historical authority—the romances, that is, and the legends and the beliefs of the people that rest only on tradition—or even so much of history as is carried about by travellers from one country to another, and is to be found only in the picturesque though often shadowy and uncertain form of—travellers' tales.

ABOUT the beginning of the fifth century, in the year 407, the country of Aquitaine was invaded by the barbarians coming from the North, and on their way to the Pyrenees Poitiers was sacked by them. A little later, in the year 419, Aquitaine and Poitiers, as its capital, was ceded by the Emperor Honorius to the Visigoths, whose rulers thus became Kings of Aquitaine. They were Arians— followers of Arius, the heretic of the fourth century, the Greek priest whose heretical doctrines were the subject of consideration at the famous conference of Nicæa, summoned by the Emperor Constantine in the year 325, and of whom one hears so much in the history of Poitiers in the time of Saint Hilary and Saint Martin of Tours—disbelievers in the mystical doctrine of the Trinity, persecutors of the clergy, and detested of the Catholic Church.

And so it happened that in the year 507 Alaric II., King of the Visigoths, was King of Aquitaine, and held his court at Poitiers. And at this time Clovis, King of the Franks, who a few years before had been converted from paganism to Christianity, was invited by the Catholics—who desired to come under his rule as a Christian king—to attack the Visigoths and drive them out of France. And Clovis, who had long desired to possess the country, sent ambassadors to King Alaric with instructions to pick a quarrel with him on some pretence or other, and to make it plain that he was determined to possess the country, and that unless it was given up to him he would attack the Visigoths at once. Simultaneously he gathered together a great army from all parts of Gaul and Germany, and Alaric put himself on his guard and strongly fortified Poitiers. It is related of King Clovis that before starting on this expedition he addressed his troops and described to them the justice of his cause—in the way he looked at it—and the wickedness of the heresy of the Arians. "Not one of you shall ever again wear a beard," he said to them, "who does not conquer these heretics and drive them out of the land."

And so the Franks took their way to Poitiers through the beautiful country of Touraine. And as they reached the city of Tours, King Clovis would not himself enter the city, but sent messengers, devout and holy men, to recommend his enterprise to God, and Saint Martin, whose shrine was in the town. And as the messengers entered the church where the citizens were at prayer, the priest, "Celluy

qui portoit la chappe," commenced at that moment
to sing the verse of the Psalms (Psalm xviii.,
verse 39), " Præcinxisti me domine virtute ad bellum,
supplantasti insurgentes in me subtus me et inimicos
meos dedisti mihi dorsum, et odientes me disperdisti,"
that is, " Thou hast girded me, oh Lord, with
strength unto the battle, Thou hast thrown down
mine enemies under me, Thou hast made mine
enemies also to turn their backs upon me, and hast
destroyed them that hate me." And the messengers
took this for a good omen, and when they had
made their offerings on behalf of the King, they
returned and told him what had happened. And the
King, who was greatly encouraged by the omen,
made a vow to God and Saint Martin that in
case he should have the victory over the Visigoths
he would, on his return to his own land, make
an offering to Saint Martin of—amongst other
treasures—his horse—his own favourite horse !

And then in the best of spirits he set forward with
his army to Poitiers. And thinking, from what he

heard on the way, that King Alaric might attempt to retreat from Poitiers to Bordeaux and so escape him, he sent forward a part of his army to Saint Maixent—a little and poor hamlet where Saint Maixent was living—that they might there close the road to Bordeaux.

And when the soldiers would have entered and pillaged the church, the saint protested, and as one of the company raised his sword and would have put him to death, the arm of that tyrant remained suspended in the air without power of movement, and presently in the sight of his companions the arm withered away, at which the rest of the soldiers who had been newly baptized wondered, and greater still was their astonishment when the saint cured that unfortunate man and his arm became whole to him again.

And King Clovis passed quickly on with the rest of his army towards Poitiers, and when they came to the village of Cenon, on the river Vienne, near the town of Chatellerault, where they proposed

c

towards the King, and passing lightly through the turbid and discoloured water on foot, without swimming, disappeared into the forest on the other side.

And the King watching the stag, and believing this to be a direct intervention of Heaven in his favour, made the whole army—more than sixty thousand men—pass through the river at that spot, where was an excellent ford. And at night he took up his quarters in the environs of the city of Poitiers, in the faubourg of Saint Hilary.

And as he slept in his pavilion, those who kept watch saw a great and miraculous light, which, coming out of the church of Saint Hilary, fell upon the King's tent and there remained, which they took to be an omen that God would, by the merits of the Saint, aid the Franks to destroy the Visigoths and restore to the country the Catholic Faith.

In the darkness of that night King Alaric left the city with his army by the eastern gate, which

C 2

is known as La Porte Joubert, intending to retreat in the direction of Bordeaux, and Clovis, being informed of his departure in the early morning, pursued him, and a great battle was fought between them at daybreak at a village a few miles northwest of the city named Vouaille, or Vouglé. The battle, which was a short but very desperate one, ended before noon. Alaric, who was brave and prudent in war, encouraged his troops and kept them in order, and they fought very valiantly, as did the Franks. At last the two kings, Clovis and Alaric, met and fought together, hand to hand, and the battle was decided in single combat between them, the rest of the armies standing by and looking on.

And Alaric was killed by Clovis, and upon the death of their leader the Visigoths fled in confusion, and the roads were strewn everywhere with their dead. The slaughter was so great that still—says Bouchet—one sees the tombs and places of burial all along the country from Vouaille, where the battle was fought, as far as Chauvigny and the river Vienne. And the Visigoths that escaped fled away into Spain, and the people of Auvergne, who were with them, hastened back into their own country ; and King Clovis remained a long time at Poitiers, and was made King of Aquitaine, and spent the winter at Bordeaux. And thus the Visigoths were ridded out of the land. On his way home King Clovis visited the shrine of Saint Martin at Tours, and, in performance of his vow, he made there an offering of his horse; but on his departure from the city a feeling of misgiving came over him that he had thus given away his friend, and he sent messengers to the monks with a proposal that they should let him have the horse again, and that he would give them for him a great deal more than his value—namely, a hundred pounds in gold. But the monks said they would not agree to it, and the feet of the horse remained immovable— miraculously glued, as it were, to the stable floor. Upon this the King sent the monks another

hundred pounds, and yet another, and a fourth and
a fifth offering, each of one hundred pieces of gold,
and at last the monks took the money—the horse's
feet were by unseen hands released from the floor
of the stable, and they let him go.

"By all the saints in Heaven," said King Clovis,
as he rode merrily out of Tours, "Saint Martin has
been a good friend to me, but he *does* make one
pay for it!" And how the monks spent the money,
or what they did with it, was never known. But to
this day the spot where the deer crossed the river
Vienne is pointed out to travellers by the people of
the country in remembrance of the story: "Le pas
de la biche," the people of the country tell you as
they point out the ford across the beautiful river.
"Le pas de la biche"—"the footstep of the hind."

Of the battle that was fought at or near Poitiers
between Charles Martel and the Saracens,
under their leader Abdérame, on a Saturday
morning in October, A.D. 732.

Of the battle that was fought at or near Poitiers between Charles Martel and the Saracens, under their leader Abdérame, on a Saturday morning in October, A.D. *732.*

RATHER more than two hundred years passed over the old city before the next battle was fought here, and that was the famous battle between Charles Martel and the Saracens under Abdérame, or Abedran, on a Saturday morning in October, in the year 732.

In the early part of the eighth century, Eudes, who was then Duke of Aquitaine, desired to throw off his allegiance to the Franks, and to assume independence, and it is thought probable that with this view he effected secretly an alliance with the Saracens of Spain. At any rate, in the autumn of 732 an enormous army of Saracens, under the command of Abedran, coming through the passes of the

D

Pyrenees, burst suddenly into France, and having quickly accumulated an immense booty, they swept forward, driving all before them, and spreading dismay and confusion through the country till they got as far as Poitiers. Here they sacked the churches of Saint Hilary and Saint Radegonde, and all that was outside the city, but the city itself they could not enter, owing to the great strength of its Roman walls. And near Poitiers they were met by Charles Martel, who was accompanied by his brother, Childebrand, and his army of Franks, and a terrific battle was fought between them at the hamlet of Moussai-la-Bataille on the banks of the Clain, a little village between the two Roman villages of Les Barres and La Tricherie, north-east of Poitiers, on the way to Chatellerault. The army of Charles Martel consisted of troops collected from France, Burgundy, Austria, and Germany. The Saracens were, according to an old tradition, four hundred thousand strong. For seven days the two armies stood fiercely watching one another, neither venturing to attack.

At length, on a Saturday morning, the battle began, and the fight lasted from sunrise till night—the more terrific on account of the unbridled fury of the Saracens, who at the end of the day were beaten, and retreated sullenly into their camp for the night; and in the darkness of the night they fled away headlong into Spain, leaving their tents standing and camp fires burning, so that Charles Martel was unaware of their flight till he was on the point of recommencing the battle the following day. Among the slain was Abdérame, their leader, who was left dead upon the field. It is recorded that more than three hundred thousand of the Saracens were slain in the battle and in the pursuit after it. Ordericus Vitalis puts the numbers that were killed at three hundred and twenty-five thousand. Bouchet puts them at even more. Thus were the Saracens driven out of France; and it was for this that the surname Martel was given to Charles—"qui merita le surnom de Martel a Charles." Nine years after this Charles Martel

died, and, according to an account in an old French
chronicle, he was buried at the Abbey of Saint
Denis, in a tomb of alabaster, amongst the kings
of France, with this inscription over him (which has
been translated from the French) :—

"After having subdued all my neighbours,
conquered Austria, Brabant and Aquitaine, and,
near Tours, slain the Saracens, four hundred
thousand of them, less twenty thousand, in the
plain, made four kings of France, and their
domain. I so fought with my good sword of
steel, that I was called of men Charles Martel—he
of the hammer—and never wishing to be crowned
a king, I took, in the year 741, an hostel at Saint
Denis, where now I lie—'en cendre.' "

And little Pepin, the son of Charles Martel,
succeeded him as King of Aquitaine, and in the year
768 he was succeeded as king by his son, the great
Emperor Charlemagne, the first Emperor of the
West.

Of the battle that was fought between Edward the Black Prince and John, King of France, on the field of Maupertuis, close to Poitiers, on Monday morning, the 19th of September, A.D. 1356.

Of the battle that was fought between Edward the Black Prince and John, King of France, on the field of Maupertuis, close to Poitiers, on Monday morning, the 19th of September, A.D. 1356.

THE third great battle of Poitiers was that fought by the Black Prince against King John of France on Monday morning, the 19th September, 1356, a few miles to the east of Poitiers, on the field of Maupertuis, now known as the farm of La Cardinerie, a little north of the beautiful Abbey of Nouaillé.

In the summer of 1356, on the conclusion of a truce that had been in force between England and France, an English army, commanded by Henry, Duke of Lancaster (father-in-law of John of Gaunt,

afterwards Duke of Lancaster, " time-honoured
Lancaster "), invaded Picardy and Artois, the
northern provinces of France.

Simultaneously the Black Prince, who was Duke
of Aquitaine, on the eve of the Translation of
Saint Thomas of Canterbury (the 6th of July), left
Bordeaux, where he had been spending the winter,
after devastating the south of France in the autumn
of 1355, with the purpose of joining the Duke
of Lancaster's army on the River Loire. And it
was intended that the two armies should march
together to Paris and there establish the claim
of King Edward III. to rule the two countries as
one kingdom, he to be King both of England and
France.

Having overrun the province of Languedoc, the
Prince, moving slowly northward, took at the beginning of August, 1356, in a night assault, by means
of scaling ladders, the city of Perigueux, about
eighty miles north-east of Bordeaux on the way to
Limoges.

On the 21st of August he reached Argenton,
and on the 22nd, with the little army that accompanied him, he reached the beautiful city—" Villa
Pulcherrima "—of Chateauroux. It was but a little
army—no more than ten thousand to twelve thousand
men, English and Gascons mixed—that accompanied
the Prince. On the other hand, the French army,
that was being led against him by King John in
person, consisted of upwards of fifty thousand men—
picked soldiers — among them the flower of the
chivalry of France.

After leaving Chateauroux on the 23rd of August,
the English army, still moving northward, reached
Issoudun on the 25th, and on the 28th arrived at
La Ferté, near the boundary of Aquitaine, where
they crossed the River Cher into the land of the
King of France. And here they attacked and put to
flight a large body of the French under the command
of Le Gris Mouton, de Chambly, who was the first to
fly. They next attacked and burnt Aubigny. Then
they rested for a day or two at Vierzon, and there

E

they heard that King John, at the head of a great army, coming against them, was in the city of Chartres, that the bridges over the River Loire were broken by the French, and that the towns that lay along its banks were closed against them, so that it was impossible for the Prince to cross the river and join the English army on the other side.

But, nothing dismayed at the news, the Prince rode west with his troops to the town of Romorantin, and took the town by assault on the 31st of August; and on the 3rd of September he took the castle (where the French had taken refuge after the loss of the town) and destroyed it by fire. " The Prince came, I assure you," says Chandos Herald, " as far as Romorantin. There he took the town by assault, and made prisoners Messire Boucicault, and the great Lord of Craon and very many others—more than two hundred were there taken—all fighting men of great valour. Rest assured I speak the truth."

The movements of the English after the taking of Romorantin, on the 31st of August, are recorded by the Monk of Malmesbury, an eye-witness of the campaign, who tells the story from day to day, and by the contemporary chroniclers, Geoffrey Le Baker of Swynebroke, and the herald Chandos (not the great English Captain Sir John Chandos, the Constable of Aquitaine, who accompanied the Black Prince throughout the campaign, and was one of the leaders of his army, but his herald, who, according to a custom of the time, took his name), and by Froissart and Jean Bouchet, the sixteenth century chronicler of Aquitaine.

From Romorantin the Prince marched north-west as far as Tours, and encamped for three or four days before the city, and burnt a part of the suburbs. Here he heard that King John had left Chartres and was rapidly advancing upon him with an enormously superior force, and in consequence of this news and being unable to cross the Loire and join the Duke of Lancaster's forces on the north side

E 2

On the 12th of September the French, having crossed the river Loire at Blois, were at Amboise; the English at Montbazon. And here Hélie de Talleyrand, the Cardinal of Perigord, came to the Prince, with a great concourse of bishops and prelates of the Church as messengers sent specially by the Pope, to bring about, if possible, an agreement of peace. The Cardinal was destined shortly to play an extremely interesting part in the events that immediately preceded the battle—and in its results.

On the 13th of September the French army was at Loches, and the English, hastening their retreat, were at La Haye. On the 14th the French, in rapid pursuit of the Prince, were at La Haye; and the English marched towards the west, and reached Chatellerault. So close were the two armies at this moment that the French entered La Haye only a few hours after the Prince had left. "As I have heard," says Chandos Herald, "the one army camped before the other, and pitched their tents so

near that, by Saint Peter, they watered their horses
at the same stream."

On the 15th of September the French, by a
forced march of thirty-five miles to the south,
arrived at Chauvigny, on the river Vienne; and the
English spent that and the next day at Chatellerault,
the Prince being in doubt which road he had better
take to get to Bordeaux. The object of this movement of the French—in marching to Chauvigny—
was to drive the Prince towards the west, and so
cut off his retreat to Bordeaux. They cared nothing
about protecting Poitiers, which they knew to be in
their favour, and in a good state of defence.

On Friday, the 16th of September, the French
king, at the head of his army, crossed the river
Vienne at Chauvigny, and advancing west towards
Poitiers, he encamped that night in the open country,
at the farm of La Chaboterie—about four leagues
distant from Chauvigny and two from Poitiers.

On Saturday, the 17th of September, the English,
starting very early from Chatellerault, after marching

south along the west bank of the river Vienne proceeded towards the field of Maupertuis. In the course of the day a skirmishing party of the English came into collision with a portion of the rear guard of the French army which had been left behind at La Chaboterie, where after a sharp fight a number of illustrious persons belonging to the French army were taken prisoners, and the French were beaten and fled. Here the Marshal of Burgundy was taken prisoner, and the Count de Joigny and the Count d'Auxerre. The ground occupied by the English that night was to the south of what is now known as the farm of La Cardinerie in the commune of La Nouaillé, near the station of Nouaillé, where the railway from Poitiers to Blanc joins the railway to Limoges, at two little leagues' distance, as the crow flies, from Poitiers.

And on that night the two armies were no more than two miles apart, yet they knew it not—so completely had they surrounded themselves with solitude by their cruel treatment of the people of

the country—for every peasant and inhabitant of
the neighbourhood had fled in terror at the
sight of them, fearing that they would be pillaged
or ill-treated, and there was no one to give them
news.   It seems probable that King John had no
reliable news of the movements of the Prince's
army after leaving La Haye.

A picturesque story is told by the chroniclers of
the French troops as they marched out of Chauvigny
on their way to the battle.   As the men passed
across the bridge over the river Vienne in the
presence of the King, who stood watching them,
they sang in chorus the song of Roland. " Poor
France," said King John, laughing at them, " Poor
France, where are your Rolands?"   " Show us a
Charlemagne," shouted a merry little Poitevin
banneret to him (Jean Janvre, surnamed Bagoulin,
or the free-speaker). " Show us a Charlemagne,
and we'll show you the Rolands!"   And the
great procession passed on singing the famous
song.   The whole of the 16th of September was

occupied by the French in crossing the bridge at Chauvigny over the river Vienne.

This story of Jean Janvre reminds one of a story of the Norman soldier Taillefer at the battle of Hastings, just three hundred years earlier than the battle of Poitiers, save ten—as told in the Anglo-Norman romance " Le Roman de Rou " ;—

> " Taillefer, ki mult bien cantout
>
> Sor un cheval ki tost alout
>
> Devant li Dus alout cantant
>
> De Karlemaine è de Rollant
>
> E d' Oliver è des vassals
>
> Ki morurent en Renchevals."
>
> —R. DE R. 13, 149.

that is—

> " Taillefer, who sang wondrous well,
>
> Rode up, mounted on a swift horse
>
> Before the Duke, singing as he came
>
> Of Charlemagne and of Roland
>
> And of Oliver, and of all the vassals
>
> Who died in Roncesvalles."

F

And as the Norman army drew near to the English, " Sire," said Taillefer to Duke William, " I have served you long, and much you owe me for that service—and to-day you shall pay me what you owe. I ask as my reward, and earnestly beseech that you will grant it, that you give me the right to strike the first blow in this battle," and the Duke said, " I grant it."

> " Otréiez mei, ke jo n ' i faille,
>
> Li primier colp de la bataille
>
> E li Dus respont :—Je l'otrei."
>
> —R. DE R. 13, 163.

And Taillefer, putting his horse to the gallop, rode out of the Norman lines towards the English, and in sight of the two armies struck an Englishman dead. And then he was surrounded, and what became of him is not known. And loud and far sounded the bray of the horns, and the shock of the lances, and the mighty strokes of the clubs, and the clash of the swords : and thus, with the song of Roland, was the battle of Hastings begun.

On the morning of the 17th of September the French king, after first marching west from La Chaboterie in the direction of Poitiers, found, when on the point of entering the city, that the English, who had that morning marched from Chatellerault, were behind him in the plain of Maupertuis, and without losing an instant, he turned his army and camped that evening right in front of the English in the plain. The French encampments that night were on the north side of the farm buildings of La Cardinerie, the English on the south.

Here the French army was arrayed in three great "battles"—that under the command of the Dauphin, the Duke of Normandy, assisted by his two brothers, the Duc d'Anjou and the Count of Poitiers, a little to the north-west of the farm buildings of La Cardinerie; that of the Duke of Orleans, brother of the King, behind that of the Dauphin; and the battle of the King, behind

that of the Duke of Orleans. The battles of
the two French marshals, the Lords Clermont
and d'Audenham, stood side by side in advance of
the Dauphin, and immediately facing the armies
of the Prince. "The French are in enormous
numbers," said the scouts, who had been sent out
by the Prince to bring him news of their position
and strength. "No matter," quietly replied the
Prince. "Dieu y ait part." And the French were
fifty thousand strong—the English ten!

During the night the armies were surrounded by
sentinels; the greatest order and a strange confidence prevailed in the English camp.

At daybreak on Sunday, the 18th of September
—it was a beautiful morning, "Aurora Dominice
lucis rutilante"—King John rose early, and had
a solemn Mass sung by the priests in his pavilion,
and received the Sacrament, he and his four sons.
And then he determined to attack the English that
day, and the army was ranged in order of battle,
the trumpets sounded, and the banners were

displayed in front of the lines in the name of God and of Monseigneur Saint Denis.

"La était toute la fleur de France, ni nul chevalier ni ecuyer n'était demeuré à l'hotel, s'il ne voulait être déshonoré."

And the King, riding on a white charger and holding a white baton, galloped from battalion to battalion and encouraged the men. And just as he was on the point of giving the signal for the commencement of the battle, there appeared before him a procession of priests coming from Poitiers, headed by the Cardinal, who besought him that he might be allowed if possible to make terms with the Prince.

"Very well," said King John, after some hesitation, "be it so, but return quickly."

And then the Cardinal and his followers hurried across to the English camp and made a similar request to the Prince. "Sire," said he to the Prince, "for God's mercy take pity upon so many noble men that this day may lose their lives in the battle. If one might make you agree, God and the Holy Trinity would take it in good part of you."

"Very well, holy father," said the Prince; "make terms if you can, but my quarrel is just and I fear nothing."

And the Cardinal, all in tears, rode back to King John and besought him to suspend the battle for the honour of God, who suffered crucifixion, and for the love of the Virgin His Mother; and with great reluctance, and contrary to the advice of some of his council, the King agreed to a truce till sunrise the following day. Upon this the French broke up their ranks and retired into their encampment for the day.

And all that day the Cardinal " chevaucha d'un camp à l'autre " trying to make terms of peace, but to no purpose. And all the time the Prince was strengthening his position every moment in the midst of the vines and the rough tangled bushes and broken ground and the marsh in and about which his little forces had been very skilfully placed. Great ditches were dug and barricades erected, and behind the hedges and the wide dyke on either side the long narrow road that led to their position stood the English archers—the men of Crècy and the Gascons, shoulder to shoulder, with the long bows that would shoot their enemies down at a distance of a hundred yards, and they were ready to shoot across the dyke at the French passing down that road—for they could go by no other—at a distance not of two hundred yards, but two or three!

But while the French had abundance of provisions, the English suffered greatly from want of food, for the surrounding country had been devastated and they had next to nothing to live on but grapes, which, happily for them, were then ripe, for the gathering in of the vintage was about to begin.

But to return to the Cardinal, who, from sunrise till dark on that 18th of September, laboured with all his strength to bring about a peace between the two armies, while the Prince spent the whole of the day strengthening his position and preparing for the battle in the midst of the vines.

A very unfortunate thing for the French was this—says the French chronicler, Jehan Bouchet— for with all these comings and goings of the Cardinal, the English were perpetually strengthening them- selves in the midst of the vineyards. If but at the first, he adds, the French, who are by nature quick, and count it nothing to gain battles by tricks and devices, as do the Italians and the Venetians and the people of Spain—if but at the first the French had attacked the English, they must have completely destroyed them, as the Black Prince himself knew very well; for he kept on making fine offers to King John, and made pretence of surrendering to him all the booty he had taken in the country; and all this was but a device to gain time! But King John should have known better; he should have known from sad experience that the perfidious English did not always keep their promises. It was not to be expected for a moment that he would ever get anything by them. At last the King told the Cardinal plainly that he was tired of his proposals; that he would have no more of them; that he would accept nothing short of the immediate and unconditional surrender of the Prince and a certain number of his companions; and that he might just go and tell the Prince so, and orders were given that the Cardinal should not be allowed admission to the French camp again; and to this the Prince quietly replied, when the Cardinal told him what had happened, that in that case the English preferred death to dishonour. And by this time his forces were occupying a very strong position indeed in the thick cover of the vines. And so the Cardinal left the Prince in great displeasure on the night of Sunday, the 18th of September, and returned to Poitiers. Both parties seem to have thought that the Cardinal was deceiving them—

> "Chascun disoit en son parti:
> 'Cil Cardinal nous ad traï'
> È las! Pur Dieu, mais noun avoit
> Car tout plorant s'en departoit
> Et chivachoit devers Paitiers."

G

I have put the story into English thus :—

"And the tears rolled down the Cardinal's cheeks,
    As sadly he rode away,
For though he had come on an errand of peace,
    Each side to itself did say,
'The Cardinal is but a traitorous friend,
    And he doth us all betray ;'
The French king said, 'He hath lost us time—
    A whole long summer day!'
'To our foes,' said the Prince, 'his suite have gone—
    I see them stealing away!'
But, by heaven! the Cardinal loved them both,
    And for peace alone did pray."

It should here be mentioned that on the failure of the negotiations of the Cardinal, several of his company—knights and men-at-arms—choosing for their leader the Castellan of Amposta, who was one of his suite, stole away from the English camp and joined the French army—an act of treachery, seeing that during the negotiations they had been allowed to see the English positions and their lines of defence. The Cardinal's nephew, the Lord Robert de Duras, was one of them. We shall see a little later what was his end.

On the eve of the battle—on that Sunday evening on which the Cardinal was using his last endeavours to arrange a peace between the armies, and the truce was still in force—the English knight, Sir John Chandos, met in the open country that lay between the two camps a French lord—the Lord de Clermont, marshal of the French army; and it happened that they both had the same device upon their surcoats—a figure of the Madonna beautifully worked in blue embroidery, encircled by sunbeams of gold.

"How dare you wear my arms!" said Lord Clermont fiercely to Chandos.

"It is you who wear mine," was the quick answer. "I shall show you to-morrow, when this truce is ended, that they are not yours, but mine."

"Oh!" said the Lord Clermont, "you English

are a dull people ; you invent nothing yourselves, but just take for your own any beautiful things you happen to see that belong to other people! This theft is just like you."

And so they parted ; and before the next evening the Lord Clermont was dead—he was shot down by an English archer very early in the fight. Bouchet, in telling the names of those who were killed in the battle, records of him, "And these are the names of those who were buried in the church of the Preaching Friars in Poitiers :

"Le Duc de Bourbon de la partie dextre du grant aultier ;

Le Mareschal de Clermont aussi de l'autre couste ; "

and side by side they rest together still—the famous Duc de Bourbon and the Lord Clermont—on either side the high altar in the church of the Preaching Friars in Poitiers.

In the early dawn of the morning of the 19th

of September—before sunrise—the Cardinal once more appeared upon the field of battle to endeavour to bring about a peace, but the French received him angrily, and dismissed him with menaces. The Prince answered him quietly : " Victory depends not on men, but where God shall send it. We are ready for the battle, and shall fight."

And as the sky reddened in the east on that morning, and the glorious sun rose slowly above the horizon over the great plain of Maupertuis, as the long shadows fell upon the grass, and the birds sang, and the flowers unfolded themselves to the sun, and the little brook ran merrily down to the river, and the white mist rose in a haze of silver from the broad surface of the marsh to the sky— these signs of peace and rest, and all the beauty of the summer day, were but as heralds of the storm — as the stillness before the tempest — the silent sweep and swirl of the waters on the verge of the whirlpool ; for as the first rays of the sun fell upon the plain the truce between the two armies came to an end, and one of the fiercest and most desperate of battles that has ever been fought was about to begin.

At sunrise, says the chronicler, "the banners and pennons of the armies were unfurled to the wind ; bright shining in gold, and azure, purple gules and ermine," and the trumpets sounded through the hosts and made the earth ring.

On that morning King John was arrayed in royal armour, and nineteen other knights were in armour exactly like his own—the better to protect him in times when personal conflict between the leaders of an army and the opposing forces was frequent.

It was thus that James IV. of Scotland was slain in the battle of Flodden Field ; and before then, in the time of Richard III., one remembers how, at the battle of Bosworth, King Richard, before losing his own life, had slain many of his enemies clothed as Richmond was—

"I think there be six Richmonds in the field. Five have I slain to-day instead of him.'

When about to take up his position for the battle, the Prince addressed first his troops generally, and then the archers of his army, in a very spirited speech. He reminded them of the great deeds of their ancestors, of the love they should have of their country, of the duty they owed to their captains; "and," said he to the archers, "if victory come to us with life, we will still continue firm friends as always we have been, but if ill fortune so wills it that we end both life and labour together here, these gentlemen, my companions, and I with them, will drink of the same cup that you do. We stand or fall together as God decrees." And then he proceeded to set his army in order for the battle. There was a hill close by, and on it a plateau, planted on the top with hedges and ditches. A pasture field was on the north slope of the hill, with many rough bushes on it. On the south side were vineyards covered with vines which just then had the force of thickets, for the vines were at their strongest before the gathering of the grapes had begun. And on the north side of the hill was broken ground and little valleys and a rivulet and a marsh. And all beyond, to the north, was the great open plain, where the French armies were.

And first a company of the English crossed the valley and took the hill and hid themselves among the rough bushes at the top. And the Earl of Warwick, with the van-guard of the army, was posted on the north slope of the hill next the marsh, facing the French. The middle-guard of the army, under the Prince, was posted to the right of the van-guard, in the rear. And the rear-guard, under the command of the Earl of Salisbury and the Earl of Oxford, was posted to the rear of the van-guard, on its left, higher up on the hill.

The ground on which the van-guard and middle-guard of the English army lay was divided from the ground on which the French armies were in the plain by the marsh and a long hedge and ditch bordering a winding road, which led up to their position through the marsh. In the upper part of

this hedge—a thick and thorny hedge—towards the brow of the hill, was a great gap, through which no more than five men could pass abreast, "ubi quinque homines armati possent introire fronte erecta et non plures," and this was led up to by the road from the plain.

To the left rear of the Earl of Warwick stood the Earl of Salisbury with the rear-guard at a distance of a stone's throw behind the gap.

The ground on which the Prince's army stood was on an adjoining hill, or rising ground, thickly covered with bushes and vines.

The archers were posted in front of the first division—the van-guard of the army—on either side the hedge and ditch that bordered the road through the marsh. Shoulder to shoulder the men of Crécy stood there with the Gascons, protected by the hedge and ditch and the other shelter they had made for themselves, during the comings and goings of the Cardinal, ready to shoot at short distance all passers down the road.

H

The battle commenced at about six in the morning when the advance-guard of the French under the two Marshals—picked men, all mounted on horses—rode at full gallop towards the gap in the hedge, on the brow of the hill, from which they proposed to attack in the rear the forces under the Earl of Warwick and ride down and trample under foot the English archers in the marsh; but on seeing what was being attempted, the Earl of Salisbury with the rear-guard of the army pressed forward to the gap and prevented all passage through it, and a fierce hand-to-hand fight ensued for the possession of the hill. And here Lord Clermont was among the first of the slain.

The French, being thus unable to pass through the gap, were fiercely shot at by the archers who lined the road that led up to it, and who had the treble protection of the hedge, the ditch and the marsh; and as the French horsemen came struggling and in disorder to the gap, the Earl of Salisbury's forces met them and slew them:

hardly any of them escaped. Then, while the confusion of the French was at its height, the Earl of Oxford moved a large body of the archers to the side of the road, with orders to shoot at the hinder parts of the horses and the horsemen, whereupon the horses fell upon their riders and ran back upon the army that was following, and the French were thrown into inextricable confusion.

At this point of the battle Lord William Douglas, who was wounded, and Lord Archibald Douglas, his brother, who were fighting with the French against the English, fled with the Scots who fought with them, from the field. Then the van-guard of the English army joined with the middle-guard and awaited the further attack of the French. And the battle of the French, under the Dauphin, came upon them and another terrible battle ensued.

"In times of old," writes the Monk of Malmesbury, "at the third or fourth or, at least, at the last of six flights of the arrows, men could tell to which side victory would incline ; but now a hundred

H 2

flights of arrows had been sent and neither side had given way. Never before was heard of such a terrible and prolonged struggle as this. And it has been said," says the Monk, " but I will not myself vouch for the truth of it, that the French saw a horseman riding through the air—in the sky—and threatening them with clenched fist as he rode! And, by the will of God, the victory remained to the English."

And in the end the French were beaten and fled, or pretended to fly, but the English restrained themselves from following them so long as the King, who lay half hid in a valley, with the rest of his armies, remained upon the field. With the flight of the Dauphin and his men, the army of the King came out and spread itself in great companies in a wide field in the plain.

Then the Prince mounted his archers on horseback and charged with an irresistible fury on the French, and a long and desperate hand-to-hand fight ensued. And one of his captains, one of the bravest and

most trusted of all his companions and his intimate personal friend, the Captal or Capitaine de la Buche, making a circuit round the hill, came unperceived upon the rear of the King's forces, and unfurling the banner of Saint George with a great cry of "Saint George for Guienne!" the archers shot into the backs and sides of the French, and the form of their battle was quite spoilt, neither could they put themselves in order or array any more.

And the French, perceiving that the royal standard with the "flouredeluces" was beaten down, fled in all directions through the fields of Poitiers towards the city, and the English followed in hot pursuit of them, and so the battle was won.

The French fled across the river Clain by the Pont Joubert, hoping there to enter the city, but the gates were shut against them by the townsmen who feared that the English might enter with them, so close was the pursuit.

With the English archers mounted on horse-back behind them, and the river, and the city

walls in front, and the closed gates, there was
no escape for the fugitives; they were struck
down and taken prisoners in all directions.
More prisoners were taken than the whole of the
English that fought with the Prince, and amongst
them King John was taken, and Philip, his son.
In the course of the day, after the defeat of the
marshals, the Duke of Orleans, with the army
under him, fled away from the battlefield without
striking a blow.

A startling incident of this great battle should
here be recorded. As the Prince, at the head
of his archers, was on the point of charging the
French after the flight of the Dauphin, he saw the
Lord Robert de Duras lying dead by the road-
side, with his banner beside him, and ten or twelve
of his men. They had all been shot down by the
English, and lay dead by the side of the road.

"Put the body of that knight on a shield," said
the Prince to his squires. "Take three of the
archers with you, and bear him away and present

him to the Cardinal of Perigord, at his house in Poitiers, with this message from me—' I salute him by this token.' "

The Lord Robert de Duras was the Cardinal's nephew and one of his suite, who had gone away to the French with the Castellan of Amposta. And this was his end !

The Constable of France was killed there, the Duke de Bourbon and the Marshal of France, the Lord Clermont, and Regnault, Bishop of Chalons, and the Lord Geoffrey de Charney, " qui portoit l'oriflame," and many others to the number of eight hundred knights, all men of renown, without counting any foot soldiers and the other horsemen, whom it was impossible to recognise among the dead.

And nearly all the French who were not killed outright were taken prisoners. Those who were slain lie buried in the convents of the Lesser Friars and the Preaching Friars at Poitiers, where the names of many of them are recorded—as many as were recognised by their friends.

The battle, which commenced about six in the morning, was ended at noon, but the pursuit and capture of the French lasted the whole of the day. In the evening, after vespers, the Prince hoisted his standard, the banner of England, on a high May tree in the midst of the battlefield. And as darkness fell upon the plain, the minstrels and the clarions and the trumpets called the troops together at that spot, and there, says Chandos Herald :

> " Lui Prince logea celle nuit
> Entre les mortz, sur le zablon
> Dedeinz un petit pavillon
> Et ses hommes tut entour luy."

The night of that great battle was spent by the English outside the city, which as yet, on account of the smallness of their forces, they did not attempt to enter ; they slept—" Entre les mortz, sur le zablon "—amongst the dead, upon the plain—the Prince and his men with him, around the standard, upon the battlefield in the open country—amid the vines—beneath the stars.

And King John and his little son, Philip—much against the will of the Gascons and the people of the South, by whom they had been captured, and who wished to retain them in France—were sent to England as prisoners by way of Bordeaux. And for nearly four years after that the French king was detained a prisoner in England while King Edward, with his power, rode through France by Picardy, Artois, Rouen, Champagne, and so to Brittany, destroying the country before him, till at last a peace was made between the two countries by the treaty of Bretigny in the month of May, 1360.

> " Et celle paix que je vous di
> Ce fut en l'an que Dieux nasqui,
> Mil trois centz ovesque sessante,
> Au temps que le rusinol chante,
> Oep jours en joli moi de May,
> Que oiseux ne sont pas en esmay."

I

That is—

"And this peace that I tell you of was made
in the year from Christ's Nativity 1360—
at the time when one hears the song of
the nightingale—in the merry month of
May—when the fear of the winter has
departed from the birds, and the time of
their singing has come."

The battlefield of Maupertuis is not visited as
much as it should be by travellers, when one considers
how easily it may be seen. It is at a distance of
less than an hour's drive from Poitiers, on the way
to Chauvigny, and the features of the country would
seem to have been little altered since the great
battle was fought, save that the vines have now to
some extent given way to other modes of cultivation. There stand the buildings of La Cardinerie,
replacing probably the similar buildings of 1356
and the ancient hamlet of Maupertuis which was
destroyed during the battle and never afterwards

rebuilt ; and no other buildings are in sight. The same narrow road is there which occasioned the great disaster to the French, and the vast wind-swept plain, with little hills or gentle elevations dotted about over it—ground that presents itself in marked contrast to the well-wooded and well-watered country a little further south, on the way to Limoges—woods where the wild strawberries grow in the greatest abundance, and where birds all but unknown to us in England are to be found.

The story of the last illness of the Black Prince—the result of a fever caught while fighting in Spain for the cause of Don Pedro the Cruel, the king of Castile—and his death on Trinity Sunday in 1376, is beautifully and pathetically related by Chandos Herald, his historian, in words some of which I have rendered out of the old French into English thus :—

I 2

"And now have I told you all the life of
the Prince in a song. Pardon me, I pray you,
if I have done so too briefly, or if I have
passed too lightly over matters that are worthy
of record. I have done the best I was able,
but truly of the life of the Prince one might make
as great a story as that of Arthur—of Alexander
—or Clarus.

"To me, the Herald—his historian—it has
fallen to make mention and record of his deeds, of
his great valour, his noble generosity, his goodness
and prudence, of his valiant and courteous bearing
as a knight. He was a true and loyal gentleman,
working everywhere and always for the public
good.

"And thus he passed away from us with a
noble ending, remembering always with a faithful
and loving heart his Creator—his God. And this
he said to his people at his departure : 'Good
sirs, for the sake of God, listen to what I now
say to you. We are here but for a time—not as

masters, but as servants. All must go the way that I am going, therefore very humbly I entreat you to pray to heaven for me.'

"Then had the Prince, so noble and true, a repentance that assuredly God of his great goodness will take him to himself and have mercy on his soul.

"For with sincere repentance he prayed for forgiveness for all that he had done amiss whilst here on earth. And so he departed. He died in the year 1376, in the fiftieth year of the reign of his father, King Edward, in the noble city of London, on the high day of the Trinity, a festival which he ever regarded with especial reverence, and kept holy all his days.

"And now let us pray to God, the King of kings, who died for us upon the cross, that He may grant him full pardon, and receive him in glory in the heavens. Amen!

"And here endeth the history of the most noble Prince Edward, which the Herald Chandos—his faithful and willing servant—has composed and recorded with loving and willing words. Amen and Amen—by Saint Charity—for each in his degree. Amen."

Thus, as the famous herald has recorded, passed away to his rest—migravit ad Deum—in the flower of his age, and the fulness of his strength, the most noble and illustrious Edward Plantagenet, Prince of Wales—the Black Prince—a figure unique in the annals of English history—in the history of the world.

As a great soldier we think of him, a wise and trusted counsellor, an accomplished, gentle and most courteous knight, and with that distinction that raises him far above and beyond the mere rank and title of princes; he was a true and noble gentleman, a true and loyal friend, happily and justly placed, in the words of his herald, as a fourth with such a trio as Arthur, Alexander, and Clarus.

He lies buried in the chapel of the Trinity in the beautiful cathedral of Canterbury, and by his own direction, the following remarkable words (which I have rendered out of the old French into English) are recorded on his tomb :—

"All ye who pass by, with closed mouth (ove bouche close), where my body reposes, Hark to what I say to you—I, who know what I say. Such as thou art, so once was I. Such as I am, so shalt thou be. Of death I thought not while I had life, for on earth I had great honours, houses, lands, and much treasure, beautiful garments, fine horses, and silver and gold. Now I am poor, and deep in the tomb I lie ; with the earth I remain. My beauty is departed, my flesh is consumed ; very narrow is my home. It would be said of me, could men see me, that never was I a man, so great is the change. Pray then for me, passing traveller, to God, who is the King of Heaven, that He may have mercy on my soul. And to all who commend me to His safe keeping, may God grant them a place in His heavenly kingdom where sorrow and suffering are no longer known !"

It is probable that at no period of his life did the great qualities of the Prince shine forth with more brilliancy, at no time was the example he set them of greater value to his countrymen, then living or thereafter to be born, than at the battle of Poitiers. There, in the midst of a hostile country, which was yet, by right, his own—for he was the sixth in direct descent from Queen Eleanor, whose ancestors, as Counts of Poitiers and Dukes of Aquitaine, had held it from the time of Charlemagne—with his little army less than ten thousand strong, distressed with long and harassing marches, and almost destitute of food, pursued by an army of more than fifty thousand men, picked troops led by the King of France, and with him the highest nobles of the land, he turned and faced his enemies in the great plain of Maupertuis. A little hill in the wide plain—hardly worthy to be called a hill, so slight was the elevation of the ground—a small tract of marshy ground between his enemies and him, a road leading to his position bordered by a hedge and ditch, and the cover of the vines and bramble bushes that grew upon the spot where he took his stand, these were all the advantages of position that the Prince had to rely upon to meet the appalling odds that were arrayed against him. Yet, with a supreme trust in a higher power and a quiet confidence in the justice of his cause, he refused to listen for a moment to dishonourable terms that were offered him by his enemies. And he won against them on that day one of the most desperate and glorious battles that has ever been known.

" Houmout—Ich diene " was his motto. Houmout (high principle, high spirit, high courage—call it what you will) was the principle that animated him throughout the fight and before it. " Ich diene " (" I serve ") was the principle he acted on when the fight was over and in all that succeeded it, when he treated the captive king and his little son with a gentleness, a courtesy, and a generosity unparalleled in the history of the world.

K

" S'accorder ne voillent cest faitz,

Je su ci tut prest pur attendre

La Grace Dieu, au voir entendre,

Car notre querelle est si vraye

Que de combatre ne m'esmaye "

were his words to the Cardinal, who was trying to bring about a peace, immediately before the battle. "I desire a respite for my men," he said, "but if my enemy will not accord it me, I am quite prepared to abide by God's will, for our quarrel is so just, that to fight even against such odds as are here arrayed against me, I am not afraid."

Later, at the supreme moment of his fate—when facing his enemies—immediately before the commencement of the battle, his words of encouragement and hope to his archers will surely for ever be remembered as long as language lasts : " If victory come to us with life, we will remain firm friends together, as always we have been. If, which God forbid, we end both life and labour together here, be sure you will have your reward. And these gentlemen, my companions, and I with them, will drink of the same cup that you do. We stand or fall together, as God decides."

Then silently, but with a confidence strange and supernatural under the circumstances, the archers—the men of Crècy—lined the road by which, in a few moments, their enemies were to attack them—and the battle began!

These are the thoughts that fill the mind as —"with hushed lips" ("ove bouche close")—standing by the Chapel of the Trinity in the Cathedral of Canterbury, we look upon the silent reclining figure of the warrior taking his rest—his hands clasped in prayer, his face looking upwards to the sky—and the air is filled with thoughts and scenes and visions of the past, and we say that the Prince is not dead but sleepeth; for he will live for ever in the pages of the history of his country. In the minds and memories and affections of his countrymen, such as he can never die.

K 2

The Tale of the traitorous Clerk of the Maire
of Poitiers, and how the city was delivered
from capture by the English by the "Miracle
of the Keys," in the time of King John,
A.D. 1202.

The Tale of the traitorous Clerk of the Maire
of Poitiers, and how the city was delivered
from capture by the English by the "Miracle
of the Keys," in the time of King John,
A.D. 1202.

IT was after the great fire that devastated the city of
Poitiers in 1085 that Gui Geoffroi, Count of Poitiers
and Duke of Aquitaine, commenced, and his son and
successor, William IX., Duke of Aquitaine—or, as he
is better known to students of Provençal literature
and poetry, William, Count of Poitiers, the famous
Crusader, troubadour and poet, the first, and, in
the opinion of some, one of the greatest of the
troubadours—finished the rebuilding and enlargement
of the finest church in the city—the Church of
Notre-Dame-la-Grande, a building that is certainly
one of the most interesting and precious of all the

buildings of the Byzantine art that are to be found in France ; and to this church hangs a story that for picturesqueness can, perhaps, hardly be exceeded by any story out of the books of the Middle Ages.

THE STORY OF "THE MIRACLE OF THE KEYS."

Pass up to the high altar of this magnificent church, and look at the statue of Our Lady that stands high above it. The statue is of comparatively modern work, a repetition of an earlier one that was destroyed by the Huguenots in the wars of religion ; but the interest of it is that the Madonna grasps tightly in her right hand, and holds in full view of the spectator, three large bright keys. The keys are bright and new-looking, intended, apparently, for presentation to the people on fête days, when the statue is carried through the town in procession among the crowds. But by the side of the figure, nearly hidden away among the offerings of gold and jewels, and hangings of velvet and lace that envelop it, are more ancient keys.

Next to nothing is told of the story in the guide-books of Joanne, nothing at all in that of Baedeker. It is partly from the early sixteenth century chronicle of John Bouchet, a citizen of Poitiers, " Les Annales d'Aquitaine," partly, as to the story of Isabel or Ysabeau of Angoulême, from the history of the Benedictine monk, " L'Art de Vérifier les Dates des Faits historiques," and partly from the ancient chronicles of Provence in the time of the trouba-dours, and from information collected on the spot, that the story about to be told has been composed.

" L'ÉVÉNEMENT MIRACULEUSE DES CLEFS."

" THE MIRACLE OF THE KEYS."

In the last days of the twelfth century—in the time of King Richard Cœur de Lion—Ysabeau (or Isabelle) d'Angoulême, the daughter and heiress of Aymer, Count of Angoulême, was by the will of the King solemnly espoused to Hugh of Lusignan—a town a little to the south-west of Poitiers—known as

L

Ugo lo Bru, or Hugh le Brun, Count of La Marche, and being a child of tender years, she remained, as was the custom of the time, in the charge of her betrothed husband's family till the marriage should take place. During the lifetime of Richard, Ysabeau was also his ward, and under his special charge and care as Count of Poitiers and Duke of Aquitaine.

A few months after his death, in April, 1199, John Lackland (Jean Sans-terre is the name he was always known by in France), who then succeeded to the throne of England, and became also Lord of Poitiers and Duke of Aquitaine, attracted by the beauty of Ysabeau, fell violently in love with her, and induced, or forced, her father, the Count of Angoulême, to give her to him in marriage, notwithstanding her betrothal to Hugh le Brun.

The young girl (she was no more than twelve years old) was then, on a fraudulent pretence, obtained by her father from her betrothed husband's family, and married to John at Angoulême by the Archbishop of Bordeaux about the month of August,

1200, and immediately after the marriage John retired from Aquitaine.

It is related in the Provençal chronicles that he rode away with his wife on horseback, hotly pursued by the friends of Hugh le Brun ; and that first he went to England and then to Normandy, living there an idle and luxurious life with the young Queen, and apparently totally regardless of what might become of his rich provinces in France.

And the great lords of Aquitaine, and the people of the country, took the part of Hugh le Brun in the bitter quarrel that then ensued between him and the King, in consequence of the abduction of Ysabeau ; and quickly the whole of the northern part of Aquitaine, and the city of Poitiers, its capital, broke out into open rebellion against John, and called upon his nephew, Arthur of Brittany, to be their ruler in his place, contending that he had the better title to the Duchy, as being the son of Geoffrey, Count of Brittany, the elder brother of the King.

L 2

And so it happened that in the year 1202 (or,
as some chroniclers say, 1200) the people of Poitiers
were in open rebellion against King John, and were
supported in their revolt by Philip, King of France,
and by the people of Brittany, whilst the people of
certain cities in the southern district of the Limousin,
and amongst them the town of Perigeux, were in
his favour, being supported, or coerced, by the
English soldiers who had been sent into the country,
and by a number of mercenary troops that had
been sent there from Brabant.

The country of Poitou was thus at this time full
of armed soldiers—some fighting for King John,
others for his nephew, Arthur of Brittany; and
orders had been given by the King to his captains
that at all hazards Poitiers must be taken ; Poitiers
having the reputation of being a fortress nearly
impregnable on account of its position and the
great strength of its Roman walls.

In this state of things, the gates of the city
being closed against the English, and the maire of

the city having occasion to transact certain business
of importance in the South, sent his clerk, an
avaricious and unscrupulous man, but a person of
great skill and understanding, to transact this business
for him in the country of Perigord—in the town
of Perigeux. And one day in the middle of Lent,
the English who held Perigeux, finding the clerk
in the town, demanded of him who he was,
whence he came, and what was his business there ;
and he answered them that he was the servant of
the Maire of Poitiers, and that he was there on his
master's business, but as it appeared that they
wanted to take the city, he would, if they would
pay him well and make it worth his while—" Silz
vouloyet luy doñer ung bõ pot de vin "—deliver
the city to them before Easter Day. And the
English believed from what the man said that he
had relations in Poitiers, and that he was really
able to betray the place to them, and they bargained
with him to deliver the town to them for a thousand
pounds of the money of France, of which they paid

him the half in advance, and the remainder was to be handed over on the taking of the town. And the clerk appointed midnight on Easter Eve, when the people of Poitiers would, as he knew, be much engaged at their prayers in the churches of the city during the Easter services; and advised them of the manner of their coming in the darkness of the night, and of the hour at which he should meet them at the city gates.

And this done he returned to Poitiers, and showed himself more attentive to his master, the maire, than ever he had been in his life. And he did this that he might the more easily deceive him when the time for the completion of his treachery should arrive, and so deliver the city into the hands of the English, and gain the reward of his crime.

And the English prepared themselves to go to Poitiers, and to be there at midnight on Easter Eve, as the clerk had directed them; and they made subtle and false devices, so that the people of the city should not suspect the object of their approach.

And at night on Easter Eve, after the gatekeepers
had closed the gates of the city, and brought the keys
to the maire, the maire placed the keys under his
pillow, as it was his invariable custom to do, and
retired to rest for the night. And as soon as he was
asleep that disloyal servant (who was able to go in
and out of his master's chamber whenever he pleased),
seeing that the maire was fast asleep, proceeded to
rob him of the keys of the gate by the moat—" la
porte de la trachée "—where he had directed the
English to be, so that he could deliver them the
keys at midnight, and enable them to enter the
town.

But the keys could nowhere be found; they
were no longer under the maire's pillow; and notwithstanding that the traitorous clerk searched the
house from top to bottom, and every secret place
and cranny in it, the keys could nowhere be found.
And this weighed heavily on the mind of the
clerk, and towards midnight he went out upon the
walls of the city and from there tossed a letter—

"Esquel il gecta ung breuet"—to the English, who were lying in wait under the walls, in which he told them that something amiss had happened, and that they must wait where they were till four in the morning, and that he would, at the hour of four, not fail of his promise to deliver the town into their hands.

And at a few minutes to four the clerk woke up his master, and told him that the gatekeepers required the keys of the gate of *la trachée* that they might open the gate. And the maire replied that it was still too early, and turned himself over and again went to sleep. And again the clerk woke him. "Sir," said he impatiently, "a gentleman of the city has business of great importance to transact immediately with King Philip, who is in a neighbouring village, and the gates must be at once opened, that he may go to the King."

And upon this the maire, believing the false story of the clerk, desired to have the gates opened; but on searching for the keys under

his pillow he found them gone, and search where
he would, they could nowhere be found. And
at this he became exceedingly frightened, and
suspecting that he had been betrayed, he commanded that the inhabitants should be summoned to
take arms and fly immediately to the walls, and that
they should make first for the gate of *la trachée*,
being that part of the walls that was most open
to attack (where there was no river). And there
through the openings of the gates the English were
seen fighting furiously among themselves under the
walls of the town.

And the poor maire, nearly bereft of his senses,
betook himself in haste, with all the principal
inhabitants of the city, to prayer to God and Our
Lady in the church of Notre-Dame. And whilst he
was praying intently, with uplifted eyes, before the
statue of the Madonna, he saw suddenly appear
between her arms the keys of the gates of the city.
And he rendered hearty thanks to God, and so did
all the people who were there with him.

M

And the report ran quickly through the city that the English were at the gates, and the bells ("le beffroy") were rung in the churches, and the inhabitants flew to arms, and went in a state of dismay to the gate of *la trachée*, and there they saw, through the opening in the gate, more than fifteen hundred of the English lying dead in heaps upon the ground, and the others standing by panic-stricken. And upon this they opened the gates and sallied forth against the English, and made all those that remained prisoners, and brought them into the town. And these on being questioned disclosed to the maire and to the inhabitants of the city who went out with him the whole of the treason and all that had occurred. They said that that morning, at the hour of four ("a l'heure de quatre heures"), there had appeared in the sky, over the southern gate of the city (*la trachée*), a Queen, clothed in the richest and most beautiful garments, whom they believed to be the Blessed Virgin, and that on either side of her were a bishop and a nun, who from their robes and appearance they believed to be Saint Hilary and Saint Radegonde (the patron saints of the city), whose bodies reposed in the town; and that the air was filled, and the sky, with armed men without number, and angels, who menaced the English with destruction, at which sight, and feeling assured that the figures in the sky were without doubt Our Lady, Saint Hilary, and Saint Radegonde, they were filled with terror and despair, and in their frenzy some of them killed themselves and others killed or wounded their companions; and those that were left were panic-stricken and yielded themselves without resistance to the people of the town. At hearing which the inhabitants and the maire with them with one accord gave hearty thanks to God and Our Lady, and went their several ways again into the city to keep the Easter feast.

And as for that disloyal and traitorous clerk, he was no more seen ("car de puis ne fut vue"); no one knows what became of him. Some said that from one of the other gates he fled away, with

M 2

outstretched neck and hands, and threw himself
headlong into the river and was drowned; others
that the devil went away with him. To this day
exactly what became of him has never been known
to the people of Poitiers.

And in memory of the miracle the citizens
have ever since made a grand and beautiful procession of all the colleges and convents around
the walls of the city at Easter. And thus the
miraculous delivery of the city has been kept in
remembrance. The procession is to be seen every
year on the morrow of Easter in Poitiers.

> " L'an mil deux cens deux comme on clame
>   Batailla pour ceulx de Poictiers
> Contre les Angloys nostre dame
>   Et les garda de leur dangiers."

It is interesting to record that in the year 1217,
a few months only after the death of King John,

Ysabeau, the Queen of England, who was then but twenty-seven years of age, was married to her first lover, Hugh le Brun, Comte de la Marche. She was known in Poitou always as La Comtesse-Reine.

In the year 1242 she and her husband the Count rebelled against Saint Louis, the King of France, their overlord, and—says Matthew Paris—they fortified their castles and ordered their plough-shares to be converted into lances and their reaping-hooks into arrows, but were beaten and had to submit "haut et bas" to all the conditions that it pleased Saint Louis to put upon them.

By her marriage with King John, Ysabeau left a son, who succeeded him—King Henry III. By her second marriage to Hugh le Brun she left a large family, amongst them a son, Adémar, who became a Bishop of Winchester. She died in 1245, and her most beautiful and impressive tomb is to be seen in a little enclosed chapel in the Great Abbey of Fontevraud (a few hours' journey only from Poitiers), about eight miles from Chinon, where crowned with her

he Story of the great Church of Notre-Dame-
la-Grande, in Poitiers, and a day-dream
of some of the early Christian Fathers, and
among them Saint Hilary, who lived in
Poitiers in the fourth century days.

The Story of the great Church of Notre-Dame-la-Grande, in Poitiers, and a day-dream of some of the early Christian Fathers, and among them Saint Hilary, who lived in Poitiers in the fourth century days.

THE summer days are not long enough here in Poitiers. There is so much to think about, so much to write about, so much to do, and yet the visitors to the city leave it too quickly, few of them remaining here more than a day.

The Church of Notre-Dame-la-Grande, as we now see it, is of the late eleventh century date, built by Gui Geoffroi, Duke of Aquitaine, and by his son William, the ninth duke, the famous crusader, troubadour, and poet, after the great fire that devastated the city in 1085; and though the date of the older church that stood upon its site (there are the foundations of at least two older buildings beneath it) is open to some question, there is an ancient tradition—and there are good grounds for believing it to be true—that the present building replaces, and partly incorporates, an earlier Christian church that was built in the middle of the fourth century by Bishop Aliphius, in the time of the Emperor Constantine.

The story of the earlier building is thus told by John Bouchet, the sixteenth century historian of Aquitaine :—

"And after Saint Nicholas, the Bishop of Myrrha, died, and it was permitted by the Emperor Constantine to the Christians to build churches where they would, provided his own image and portrait was set up outside them, Aliphius, the Bishop of Poitiers, erected a church in that city in the name of Saint Nicholas, for in those early times it was the custom that if any one suffered martyrdom, or if any doctor of great renown died, churches were dedicated to them by name. And it is thus that the

Church of Saint Nicholas came to be built, and it
is a very ancient church and a large, and before it is
the image and portrait of the Emperor Constantine.
And at the present time" (about 1510), says Bouchet,
"it is called the Church of Notre-Dame-la-Grande,
to distinguish it from its more ancient names
of Saint Nicholas, and afterwards Notre Dame
l'Ancienne.   At one time it belonged to the
'chanoines reguliers'—monks of the Order of Monseigneur Saint Augustine—and now the 'chanoines
seculiers' are there ; and its name was changed from
Saint Nicholas to Notre-Dame on account of a
miracle that was performed in it by our Lady the
Blessed Virgin, and it has borne her name ever
since."

The building (though the interior of it is unfor-
tunately disfigured by much garish and coarse
decoration) is one of the finest possible examples of
the Romanesque art to be seen anywhere.   It is
probable that in no other building is the rich fancy
and marvellous skill of the Byzantine sculptors to

be seen to such advantage as in the great west
front of this most striking and beautiful church.

Whilst taking a first look at the west front of
the church, it may not be out of place if one calls
to mind what a French writer (Vitet) has said, in a
passing comment, on Byzantine art, in the time of
the Emperor Justinian and later :—

" In this new shape (Byzantine), which in truth
causes the exclusive admirers of antique purity to
shudder, but, nevertheless, is entitled to the more
indulgent praise of the true lovers of the beautiful,
the genius of the old Greek architects awakened ;
less correct, less severe than before, but brilliant
with youth and life, more daring, more marvellous.
For the second time the Greeks seized dominion
over the grand and beautiful art of architecture : it
was from them the Arabs received the secret of it ;
it was by them that its first lessons were imparted
to the whole of Europe."

I was five weeks in Poitiers, and every day, with
the assistance of a powerful glass, examined minutely,

and with ever-increasing interest, some portion of the building, the whole west front of which is, from the ground to the top of the gable, or pignon, literally apparelled in pictures in stone.

Many of these are late eleventh and twelfth century work of the Byzantine workmen, others replacements of sculptures that have gone, but in the same taste, and most of them very ancient. It is said that originally they were all more or less coloured—and the conical turrets of the church also—in colours and gold.

What are called the "objets de fantaisie"—the grotesques—are especially interesting, and the many little conical towers of the building, with tiles of fish-scale pattern. Amongst other sculptures, Adam and Eve are there in the Garden of Eden, and the serpent entwining the tree, and Nebuchodonozor, as the French of the twelfth century called him, in all the glory of his court, his name inscribed beneath him. Belshazzar's Feast is there, and the handwriting on the wall.

And the four Prophets are represented, and there are pictures of the fulfilment of the prophecies. The first of them is a beautiful picture of the Annunciation. Here the heavenly messenger, the angel in purple, is represented with long wings bent, as though he had just alighted, and in his right hand he holds a lily, the emblem of his mission to the mother of our Lord.

Then one sees a representation of the meeting of Mary and Elizabeth; the little house in Nazareth is shown, and, at a distance, the walls and towers of Jerusalem, and in the country between Jerusalem and Nazareth, Mary and Elizabeth meet and embrace one another, and it should be noticed that these and other figures are clad in twelfth century costumes.

Then there is a very charming representation of the Nativity—the ox and the ass gazing at the Child. The head of the ass is particularly touching, and by the side of the cradle the Virgin, from her long bed, extends her hand to the Child. Then one sees two women stooping over a little font of twelfth century construction, in which the Child has been immersed, with an aureole around his head, and above is the figure of the Cross.

There is a figure of Joseph in a magnificently embroidered dress, and allegorical representations of Mercy and Truth. Mercy is shown as a male figure, Truth as a young girl, and behind her flies away a wolf with a long tail between his legs, that ends in a flourish in the form of an acanthus leaf. And then the sight is lost in a bewildering confusion of arabesques. Above are figures of Saint Hilary and Saint Martin of Tours, and the twelve Apostles. The Mystic Lamb is there, and much of the Bible story.

There is a picture of the Ascension, and at the feet of the Saviour are the bull, the eagle, the angel, and the lion, the symbols of the Evangelists, and stars, marguerites, and fantastic animals of every kind and description. Salamanders or lizards are to be seen on the wall, basking in the sun, leaves, plants, Byzantine-headed columns great and small, fruit,

o

flowers, great wreaths of foliage, garlands of vine leaves, mingled with grapes, and here and there, apparently gazing with fixed and dignified glance at all this wonderful work of the Byzantine sculptors, conceived with a wealth and richness of imagination that is totally bewildering—here and there gazes at all this the reclining figure of a sphinx. And, lost in wonder at the work, one is set thinking as to how far the artists of Byzantium in the days of the Roman Emperors may have worked from Egyptian models, and in imitation of the art that came to them from Persia, and from many countries other than their own.

It should be noticed that in the picture of the Annunciation, in the sculptured stone, the Virgin is represented as wearing *pointed shoes*, and to these hangs a very curious story that is thus told by a contemporary historian (Ordericus Vitalis), the Saxon monk, in his history of England and Normandy, written at the end of the eleventh and early in the twelfth century:

"In the year 1089, Fulk le Réchin—or the Quarreller—Count of Anjou (the great-grandfather of Henry II., King of England) married the beautiful Bertrade de Montfort, the daughter of Simon de Montfort, and four years later she eloped from him and married Philip, King of France. Fulk had deformed feet, and in order to conceal the deformity he had shoes made of unusual length and very pointed at the toes. And the new fashion quickly became common throughout the West, a fashion which," says Ordericus, "all the world, both rich and poor, are greatly taken with. While in former times shoes with round toes, fitted to the foot, were in common use both by rich and poor, by clerk and lay, now the people insert their toes in things like serpents!"

Thus the fashion of pointed shoes came into the world through Fulk le Réchin at the end of the eleventh century.

And so the Byzantine workmen who were just at that time building the west front of Notre-Dame-

O 2

la-Grande, represented in this, as in the manner of her robes, the Virgin wearing the pointed shoes! —souliers à la pontaine—a fashion that lasted afterwards for about three hundred years.

And while looking at the pointed shoes of the Madonna, one remembers that William IX., Duke of Aquitaine and Count of Poitiers, by whom this church was built, and who reigned over Poitiers and the country of Aquitaine for forty years, beginning in 1086, just when the building was commenced, married, as his first wife, Ermengarde, daughter of Fulk le Réchin, the inventor of these shoes.

It may not improbably have been out of compliment to this lady, Fulk's daughter, that the Madonna was represented by the Byzantine workmen in shoes of her father's invention and of the newest fashion, perhaps like her own.

Sometimes—as the mood takes one—one can see far better and more clearly with closed eyes; and one hot September morning, after a closer examination than usual of the church, and having

carefully read in the old books—and especially in Bouchet—the history of the more ancient building from the time of Constantine, and the history of the city and the many interesting people that lived in it, or that were closely connected with it, throughout the fourth century, I sat down on a bale of linen under the cool awning of a linendraper's shop facing the west end of the church, and, being well out of the way of the throngs of people that were going to and from the market, began to think out how, when, and why the beautiful building in front of me, and the earlier building that it replaces, came to be there. For it cannot be doubted that the interest of any ancient building is added to a hundredfold if, when looking at it, or thinking of it, one peoples the air, as it were, with its story, and sees in imagination, yet just as plainly as if they were actually present to the eye, persons —the actual persons—and things that in the course of its existence the building would itself have seen had it had eyes.

In this frame of mind, with closed eyes, and under the cool shade of the awning, about the hour of noon, I began a day-dream.

And first out of the surrounding air there appeared on horseback the great Emperor Constantine. And before the Emperor was erected the " Labarum " or Standard, that commemorates his conversion to Christianity, and on it was the miraculous monogram and the cross, the famous trophy of the cross ; the same cross, the same trophy to which two centuries later a bishop of Poitiers—who must have seen continually the statue in front of the church, and just where I was then sitting—addressed one of the most beautiful hymns that has ever been written, the famous " Pange, lingua " of Fortunatus. And these are the words of the hymn as they came to me in my dream :—

" Pange, lingua gloriosi prælium certaminis,
  Et super crucis tropæo dic triumphum nobilem,
  Qualiter Redemptor orbis immolatus vicerit.

De parentis protoplasti fraude facta condolens,
Quando pomi noxialis morsu in mortem corruit,
Ipse lignum tum notavit, damna ligni ut solveret.

Hoc opus nostræ salutis ordo depoposcerat,
Multiformis proditoris arte ut artem falleret,
Et medellam ferret inde hostis unde læserat.

Quando venit ergo sacri plenitudo temporis,
Missus est ab arce Patris natus orbis conditor,
Atque ventre virginali carne factus prodiit.

Vagit infans, inter arcta conditus præsepia
Membra pannis involuta virgo mater alligat,
Et pedes, manusque, crura stricta cingit fascia.

Lustra sex qui jam peracta tempus implens
    corporis,
Se volente, natus ad hoc, passioni deditus,
Agnus, in crucis levatur immolandus stipite.

Hic acetum, fel, arundo, sputa, clavis, lancea
Mite corpus perforatur, sanguis, unda, profluit
Terra, pontus, astra, mundus, quo lavantur flumine.

Crux fidelis, inter omnes arbor una nobilis,
Nulla talem silva profert, flore, fronde, germine,
Dulce lignum, dulces clavos, dulce pondus sustinens.

Flecte ramos arbor alta, tensa laxa viscera,
Et rigor lentescat ille quem dedit nativitas,
Ut superni membra regis miti tendas stipite.

Sola digna tu fuisti ferre pretium sæculi
Atque portum præparare nauta mundo naufrago,
Quem sacer cruor perunxit, fusus agni corpore."

It is probable that the second line in the opening
verse, "Et super crucis tropæo," refers directly to
the standard, the trophy of the cross of Constantine.

Word by word I repeated slowly in my dream
the whole of that magnificent hymn, and saw

clearly, with closed eyes, the still figure of the Emperor on horseback—his head thrown back, and looking upwards—his hand pointing to the sky; and as the bright sunshine fell upon the square it threw upon the ground a shadow—the dark shadow of the cross.

Then, as the music of the hymn died softly away, and the vision of the Emperor and the standard passed from me, there appeared in my dream, as clearly as if they were persons actually present, Saint Nicholas and Saint Hilary, and that Greek priest who endeavoured to unsettle and disturb the Christian faith, of which Saint Hilary (the most renowned doctor of all the clerks of Gaul) was the great and principal supporter in his time—the Greek priest Arius, a man more remarkable, we are told in the old chronicles, for the elegance and beauty of his person than for his virtue; more covetous by far of worldly glory than the truth.

And then there opened out a vision of the beautiful country of Asia Minor, and that great

P

scene at Nicæa by the Ascanian Lake, where the
bishops were assembled in conference in the year
325, by the Emperor Constantine's order, to consider
and pass judgment on the Arian heresy concerning
the mystical doctrine of the Trinity. The doctrine
of the Trinity in Unity was a matter that Arius
and his followers refused to assent to, and it
is still a matter that is far from clear to the
understanding of some people. The difficulty that
that vast multitude of bishops met at Nicæa to
put an end to has never yet been satisfactorily
solved.

And then I could see in imagination—yet as
plainly as if that conference of bishops were being
then held in the square—Saint Nicholas advancing
boldly to the heretic Arius, and giving him, in the
presence of the whole council, a sound box on the
ear! "Sainct Nicolas evesque de Myrrhe oyant au
concille de Nicee que Arius blasphemoit la Trinité
inflammé du zelle de la foy bailla ung grand soufflet
a Arius en plain concille"—for which the Greeks

Pl. XI

took away from him his mitre for some considerable time!

Then appeared the figure of Saint Martin of Tours, the friend and companion and disciple of Saint Hilary, and an inhabitant of this city; and then a vision of the marriage of Saint Hilary to a lady of noble birth and large fortune of Poitiers; and the death of Saint Nicholas, a confessor of great renown; and the building of this church in his honour. Not improbably the esteem in which Saint Nicholas was held by Aliphius, the good Bishop of Poitiers (the builder of the church), and by Saint Hilary, was to some extent attributable to the punishment he administered to Arius at Nicæa—the boxing his ears!

And so the building began, and as it went up storey by storey, Saint Hilary, and his friend, Saint Martin of Tours, and Bishop Aliphius and Hilary's daughter Apre, watched it.

From the ends of the earth, we are told, people came to Poitiers to hear the wisdom of Saint Hilary, the most famous in his time of all the Christian fathers and all the clerks in Gaul.

And then there went silently by as shadows a little group of monks—the " chanoines seculiers " of the Order of Monseigneur Saint Augustine, and they looked sadly and reproachfully at the beautiful building that once had belonged to them, but it was taken away.

And then, the building being still unfinished, came the passing away of the Emperor Constantine, and the accession of his degenerate son Constans to the Empire of Italy and Gaul, who, inoculated with the Arian heresy, drove Saint Hilary into exile, and persecuted Saint Athanasius, the immortal, the Bishop of Alexandria, who at the council of Nicæa was the foremost champion of the Catholic faith, standing side by side with Bishop Nicholas at the head of the bishops who there opposed the heretical doctrines of Arius and his party; and with this the words of the wonderful creed that bears the name of Athanasius, though by him it was not written, passed with a great sweep of magnificent declamation through my mind.

Whatever else may be thought of it, few will deny that the creed is a masterpiece of style and composition. Magnificent in its clearness and beauty and strength of expression—it does one good to pass the words of it—the splendid sweep of words— through the mind without attempting to explain or understand in any hard or strictly literal sense that which to the human mind is, as the creed itself says, "incomprehensible"—great truths that can only be seen as through a mist, darkly, as alone so many of the greatest truths of the Christian faith are to be seen.

In these more quiet times the Athanasian creed may appear to some, according to their own way of regarding it, to be too intolerant. In times of old when the early fathers of the Church were fighting for the very life and breath of the Christian religion, the creed was probably a definition of faith of the utmost value exactly suited to the spirit and temper of the times—a rallying cry—a battle song.

of Saint Hilary in Phrygia, his enforced separation from his wife and daughter, and his touching letters while in exile to Apre. And I seemed to hear, notwithstanding all the noise of the market, some portions of the beautiful hymn, or oraison, written for Apre by her father, which he asked her to repeat every morning and evening of her life :—

Resplendissant largiteur de lumiere
Tu es celluy dont le sermon divin
Apres le temps de mort cruelle et fiere
Nous monstrerons le jour qui est sans fin.

* * * *

Tu es l'estoille et non celle petite
Qui est du jour advenir messaigere
Sur les humains refulgent.

* * * *

Tu es l'estoille avant le luminaire
Plus grand et cler que luysant soleil.

* * * *

And the hymn ends thus :—

Cest tout lespoir de ceste ame priante

Ce sont les veuz quelle te rend et faict

Que du matin sa lumiere poignanté

Soit en la nuict garde de tout son faict.

    •   •   •   •

Gloire a toy soit O dieu pere et seigneur,

Gloire a toy soit O Jesus filz unique,

Gloire a toy soit le vertus lenseigneur

De sainct esprit fontaine vivifique.

Then there passed all too quickly by the scene of the return of Saint Hilary from his exile in Phrygia, and the death of his wife and of Apre, who, happily for them, went before him ; and their souls, we are told, were borne to heaven by the angels—"La pucelle Apre trespassa et fut son ame portée en cieulx par les anges."

Then passed through my mind the remembrance of Saint Hilary's friendship with Saint Just and

Pl. XIII.

Saint Lienne, and the scene of his death in the ancient house belonging to him—" L'Oratoire de la Celle " (afterwards a monastery known as Saint Hilaire de la Celle), not far from where I was thus dreaming in his city of Poitiers.

On the 13th day of January, A.D. 372, Saint Hilary, feeling his departure to be approaching, sat with Saint Just and Saint Lienne, his hands folded in prayer and his eyes uplifted to the sky, the whole of the day, and Saint Just and Saint Lienne remained in prayer with him. And at night —at the hour of eleven—Saint Lienne went out at his request to see if there was any noise in the city, or if all was still; and when he returned, he said that there was still some little stir in the city, for all the inhabitants had not yet retired to rest. A little before midnight he went out again to see if all was silent, and at the hour of midnight he returned and reported that everything was still.

And at that moment there suddenly burst upon

Q

the room a light so brilliant that the standers-by could not endure to look upon it, and from minute to minute, as the light diminished, the life of the Saint ebbed gradually and peacefully away, and at the end of half an hour—with the departure of that strange light—he rendered his soul to God.

"Ita beatus Hilarius," says Fortunatus, his historian, "Ita beatus Hilarius, cum gloria migravit ad Christum, terra plorante, cœlo gaudente, eodem Jesu Christo prestante, cui cum Patre et Spiritu Sancto vivat et regnat Deus in sæcula sæculorum." That is : And so the blessed Saint Hilary in glory passed away to Christ—the earth weeping, the heavens rejoicing, and he with Jesus Christ, who with the Father and the Holy Spirit lives and reigns as God in Heaven for ever and ever. Amen.

With the gradual fading away of that light, I awoke from my dream. As shadows slowly passed from me the figures of Saint Hilary, Saint Just, and Saint Lienne.

"Monsieur dort?" said the linendraper quietly, as he passed by me in search of his goods.

"Yes," I said; "I am very tired. There is so much to see in that building, and there are so many people to-day in the square." And he thought I meant the people in the hot, noisy, crowded market, but I had seen nothing of them. The people I had seen under his awning (but this I did not tell him) were the Emperor Constantine and Saint Athanasius, Arius the heretic, Saint Nicholas and his friend Aliphius, the builder of this church and Bishop of Poitiers, the bishops assembled in conference in the plain of Nicæa, by the beautiful Ascanian Lake, Saint Hilary, Saint Martin of Tours, Saint Just and Saint Lienne, and the Lady Apre.

And then I walked quietly away into the pretty garden of the University of Poitiers—not that university that was founded and endowed by Saint Hilary in the days of his youth, about the year 324, when from all countries young people flocked to him at Poitiers to be instructed in learning and

Q 2

in the Christian faith, for that has long since disappeared; but the university that now exists, continues and carries on the great work of education in the city that was first founded by the saint. It was just when Saint Hilary had completed this university that the peace of the Church began to be disturbed by the Arian heresy, a trouble that was destined to make him famous, and it lasted his life.

Saint Hilary is the patron saint of Poitiers jointly with Saint Radegonde, and to him has been attributed, by some rightly or wrongly, the authorship of perhaps one of the finest hymns that ever were written, the "Te Deum laudamus." Volumes have been written upon the subject of this most impressive and magnificent hymn and its authorship, yet no one can pretend to say with any kind of certainty who actually composed it. Its *earliest* known *title* (in an eighteenth or nineteenth century manuscript now at Münich) is "Hymnus quem S. Hilarius *primus* composuit." And in a tenth century manuscript is

written " in Dei palinodia quam composuit Hilarius Pictaviensis episcopus." In a ninth century manuscript it is stated that the hymn was "built," by Saint Augustine or Saint Ambrose (Hymnus quem S. Ambrosius et S. Augustinus invicem condiderunt). The earliest known *text* of the hymn is an Irish version of the seventh century (from the Bangor Antiphonary) which begins with the words—not in the form in use in the Prayer Book—"Laudate pueri dominum, laudate nomen domini, Te Deum laudamus," etc. At any rate the hymn appears undoubtedly to have been written very near to the time of Saint Hilary, and in this his own city, the scene of his great work, one likes to think that it is *his*—that it was written for us by him in Poitiers.

The Story of the Benedictine Abbey of Montierneuf, built by Gui Geoffroi, Duke of Aquitaine, A.D. 1075. And some account of the great market of Poitiers, A.D. 1896.

The Story of the Benedictine Abbey of Montierneuf, built by Gui Geoffroi, Duke of Aquitaine, A.D. 1075. *And some account of the great market of Poitiers,* A.D. 1896.

To-DAY (Saturday) is the great market day in Poitiers, and on the way down to the river—first to the churches of Saint Pierre and Saint Radegonde, and then by the riverside and the mills, and past the botanical gardens to the Abbey of Montierneuf—I was detained in the market, always one of the

brightest and prettiest spots in a city of France. And
in the market-place in the square of Notre-Dame-la-
Grande a great sea of white caps of many picturesque
forms and exceeding whiteness surged around the
building, and a merry chattering of voices filled the
air ; and out of this sea of white—rising straight
out of it—stood out hard and clear the dark form
of the great church. Above it the clear blue sky
only and the sun, for it is a day of a thousand
— a magnificent summer day. From the pretty
conical turrets and bell towers on the top of the
building, one heard,' in competition with the Babel
of voices below, the light merry laughter—a ripple
of laughter—of the little jackdaws.

The great market of Poitiers is one of the
prettiest in France—full to-day to overflowing with
fruit, flowers, vegetables, fish and fowl of every
description and the finest quality. Fish fresh from
the Aquitanian sea, venison from the forests of
Gascony, the finest white broccoli, salads of all kinds,
artichokes, the finest plants of celery, white mush-

rooms, red tomatoes, melons of all colours, great and small, peaches, nectarines, figs, grapes (white and purple), pears, plums of all colours, and myriads of wild strawberries, sold in long, flat, low little baskets, of a pattern that seems to belong specially to Poitiers. The strawberries in this wild profusion are the result of the warm rain and hot sunshine of the last three or four days, and come out of the woods.

To-day the market overflows on all sides into the square. There is not room inside the large covered building for the half of it. High against the walls of the houses one sees the white broccoli and fine savoy cabbages, and hundreds of melons piled in picturesque profusion. A delightful old lady, with a black lace cap and loose flying ribbons, was sitting apart in a corner of the square quietly dozing under her umbrella—a dreamer of dreams— surrounded by and almost embedded in her great possessions of heliotrope and bright flowers, pinks, fuchsias, roses, sweet-scented stocks, and fine mari- golds. Under an umbrella of dazzling scarlet, on a strong pole let into the ground, large enough to cover a dozen people, a merchant of umbrellas was selling his wares, a little admiring crowd around him. His way of doing business is this: he produces from his stock an umbrella, neatly folded up—fine looking and slim—and this he quietly unties; then, with the rapidity of lightning, and many twirls, he flourishes it with a shriek and many gesticulations, and a face flushed scarlet with excitement—as if he were intending to personate all the fury of a storm—in the faces of the audience—now inside, now out—backwards and forwards. Then he pauses for a moment to show it, with an expression of sadness and pity on his face, in a state of absolute and apparently hopeless collapse—inside out. Then, with a serious business look, he shakes it with one twist of the wrist into proper shape again, ties it up gently, and offers it, with many smiles and the utmost politeness, to anyone who will take it of him at the very modest price, for such an article, of two francs!

There are many trades going on in the market—sellers of little wax candles and wax images for the churches, sellers of boots, shoes, hats, clothing of all kinds—everything may be found there that is required by any inhabitant of Poitiers. The ladies of the town come to the market every morning, but especially on Saturdays, with a maid or two in attendance with large baskets, and return with their supplies. There are one or two indifferent flower-shops in the town, but I cannot call to mind at the moment any shop in which vegetables are sold, unless in a chance and very small way. Practically nearly all the supplies of the city seem to be bought in the great open market around the church of Notre-Dame-la-Grande.

The market of Poitiers, in September at any rate, is remarkable too for its birds. In France one may go for days together through the country without seeing a blackbird, a thrush, a skylark, a robin, a hedge-sparrow, or a wren, and it is so with most of the birds that are common with us in England. Either they exist not or are hidden away in certain places. To the ordinary traveller through the country they are not to be seen. As a matter of curiosity I have been all over Poitiers on the look-out for that commonest of all English birds, a sparrow. Not one single sparrow was I able to find.

But birds that are very rare with us in England — extinct, or nearly so — seem to be common in this country. A day or two ago I saw a bird lying in the hall of the inn that the landlady said was "la petite outarde" (the lesser bustard), and since then I have seen this beautiful bird on the stalls of the marketwomen with partridges and quails. It is common, they say, in the country at this time of year. One was sent up for dinner a day or two ago, dressed in all its fine feathers, as one would dress a peacock in England. I bought two fine specimens of these birds, male and female, from a naturalist in the town, the male with a beautiful white frill, that hangs upon him like the chain of an alderman. And in the same shop were some pretty specimens of the birds they call "les combattants" (ruffs and reeves), birds almost extinct in England, yet quite common here. I also brought away an exceedingly pretty little nest of "les fauvettes de réseau" (the reed-warbler). It is open at the mouth —not domed over, as a wren's—and supported by three long, firm, straight stalks of the reeds.

The country of Aquitaine swarms with partridges, quails, and hares, and one sees pheasants occasionally, and certain birds are always to be seen here, "tous les jours et partout"—the magpies, the crows, the rooks and jackdaws—all birds of mischief —birds of the Middle Ages—Chaucer's birds—the "crow with voys of care. The chough the thief, and eke the jangling pye. The eel's foe, the heroune."

Eels there are in the market, little and great, this morning, and also the "herounes"—the herons, the stately fishermen of the waters of Aquitaine, that feed on the eels. Fish of every kind one sees from the Aquitanian sea at the Ile de Ré and La Rochelle.

Two of the citizens of Poitiers are always a source of considerable amusement—they are artists in black and white. In the morning the charcoal seller, "le charbonnier"; in the evening, "le marchand des journaux," the newspaper boy.

In the early morning the charbonnier arrives from the country, probably out of the forests of Gascony or the Limousin, where the charcoal is made, his little donkey-cart full of sacks of charcoal in sticks the thickness of a broomstick or smaller, the shape and colour of liquorice, and these are measured out to his customers in a round wooden measure, as one would measure a feed of corn. Man, cart, donkey, harness, are thickly begrimed with charcoal smoke, all coloured alike. And the charbonnier carries a small horn. "Toot, toot!"—he sounds two notes sharply and peremptorily as he marches down the street, looking right and left for customers on the way. Presently he stops at the door of some shop and utters, in a shrill voice, the single word "Charbonnier!" At this the donkey

s

stops instantly, and the woman of the house appears; the two exchange looks without speaking, certain sticks of charcoal are quickly measured out, handed over, and some copper coins given in exchange, and the silent party goes on its way sadly and slowly down the street. " Toot, toot! "—the customers know of the approach of charcoal only by the sound of the horn—there is no conversation over the buying and selling. The only two sounds I ever heard from the seller of charcoal were the " toot toot! " and the one word "charbonnier." A very different person—a little person—is the marchand des journaux. In the evening he appears in the streets, a merry little fellow clothed in white with a large flat Basque flannel cap on his head, and carrying a horn like the charbonnier, and on it he plays, not two notes only, but a flourish of music, to announce his arrival in the square—and there he calls out with great rapidity the names of his papers from various cities between Paris and Bordeaux. " P'tit Pr'vençal," he shouts,

"L'Venir de Vienne; who'll buy the Petit Journal de Provence and the Avenir de Vienne"—he clips his words very short and utters them very quickly, in a way that reminds one of the old Provençal poetry of the twelfth and thirteenth centuries, in the gay times of his ancestors the troubadours.

"Be m platz lo gais temps de pascor,"

"Much pleases me ever the gay time of the spring."

> "Ab l'alen tir vas me l'aire,
>   Qu'en sen venir de Provensa."
> "With my breath I drink the air,
>   The sweet air of Provence."

Truly he would have made an excellent page or Jongleur had he lived in the olden times of the troubadours, that bright little comic actor the newspaper boy.

At last, thinking of Diane and Joan of Arc, Charles VII., and Le Grand-Prieur d'Aquitaine, and of the famous English knight John Chandos, who was Seneschal of Poitou, and the adversary of Duguesclin, and others of the many people of the thousand years from the fourth to the fourteenth centuries that are with one always in Poitiers, I came at last to the river Clain, at the foot of the hill, by the gate known as La Porte Joubert—that gate where the French were massacred in thousands when, flying from the Black Prince, they attempted to take refuge in the city of Poitiers after the battle of Maupertuis. It was at this spot that the inhabitants of Poitiers shut the gates of the city against their own troops flying in confusion from the English after the battle, fearing that, unless they did so, the English would enter the city with them. Here, with the closed gates in front of them, the river immediately behind them, and the English archers mounted on horseback, elated with victory, at their heels, the French troops were either drowned in the river or cut down at the city gate, their friends not daring to let them into the city, and witnessing their destruction from the walls.

From the middle of the bridge, "Le Pont Joubert," one gets a good view of the beautiful winding river, up and down, as it flows south through the

forests towards Limoges, north towards Chatellerault and Chinon, with its clear water—deep pools and long shallows—bordered on the one side by gardens running down to it, on the other lined to-day with white-capped washerwomen, such as one knows so well from Calderon's pictures, or R. P. Bonington's, both of them English painters much esteemed in France.

The walk from this point by the river-side to the ancient Abbey of Montierneuf, past the great College of Saint Joseph and the Sacré-Cœur, and then the Botanical Gardens, is a very delightful one. Soon after passing the Gardens, one sees suddenly in the air the flying buttresses of the Abbey, to me—by reason of the close connection of its builder with the history of the Manor of Tangley, in England—work I was much engaged upon in those summer days at Poitiers —one of the most interesting buildings in Aquitaine. And this is the story of the Abbey of Montierneuf.

In the year 1058, Gui Geoffroi, Duke of Aquitaine and Count of Poitiers, succeeded—after the deaths of his two brothers, Guillaume le Gros and Guillaume le Hardi, without issue—to the Duchy of Aquitaine. His father was Guillaume le Grand, a great and powerful prince, who lived much in Poitiers, and was one of the most accomplished scholars of his time. He possessed in his library here, among other famous manuscripts, a manuscript written in letters of gold, that had been sent him as a present by the King of England—Canute—and that is said to have had a material bearing upon the life of St. Martial and the earlier history of the city of Poitiers.

Having succeeded to the Duchy in 1058, Gui Geoffroi engaged in many wars, and firmly established the great power and prestige of his country, which had suffered much in the times of his brothers. In 1060 he beat the Sire de Lusignan in a great battle. In 1062 he reconquered Saintonge from the Count of Anjou. In 1063 he subjected Gascony to his rule, and a little later he took an active part in the defeats of the Moors by the Christians in Spain.

In 1068 he captured from Geoffrey le Bel and Fulk of Anjou, the country of Saumur.

In the same year (1068) he married Aldearden of Burgundy, and, not long afterwards, Pope Gregory VII. was set in motion by Goscelin de Parthenay, the Archbishop of Bordeaux, to declare this marriage void on account of affinity—parenté—the parties being within the prohibited degrees of relationship. Pope Gregory, who was just at this time enforcing the laws of marriage very severely throughout Christendom, and removing married priests from their duties, forbidding people to listen to their masses, felt bound to take serious notice of the disregard of the marriage laws by the Duke of Aquitaine, and curiously enough the difference that arose between the Duke and the Pope on this question gave rise to the building and endowment of this very famous and beautiful church.

On his attention being called to the Duke's marriage by the Archbishop of Bordeaux, Pope Gregory submitted the question to the considera-

Poitiers for the benefit of the Benedictine Order of Cluny," a step which Pope Gregory well knew would be one of the most powerful means of enabling him to effect the reform and well-being he desired of the clergy. Cluny itself had been founded and endowed by the Duke's great ancestor William le Pieux.

And the Pope accepted the promise that the abbey should be built, but he would have none of the concessions as to Aldearden that the Duke desired in exchange. And so it came about that the building of the beautiful Abbey of Montierneuf was commenced in the year 1075, the *new* monastery on the banks of the river, by the mills of Chasseignes.

In the same year, while the building was going on, Philip, King of France, came to Poitiers to see the Duke, and to obtain, if possible, a promise of his assistance in a war with which he was then threatened by the King of England, William I. And this was just at the time when King William, having suppressed the terrible revolt of the Earls Roger and

T

January, 1082, the Prior and monks of Cluny took possession of the Abbey, which was consecrated (after the Duke's death) by Pope Urban in 1096 at a grand and splendid state ceremony, whilst he was engaged in preaching throughout the country the first crusade.

On the 24th September, 1086, Duke Gui Geoffroi died, "alla de vie à trespas," at his castle of Chize, and was buried in this, his Abbey of Montier-Neuf. He left two sons, William—who was Duke of Aquitaine and Count of Poitiers after him, the crusader, troubadour, and poet—and Hugues Hamon, who went as a crusader to the Holy Land.

In the body of the church, immediately to the right of the entrance doors, stands a raised sarcophagus of stone, the Duke's tomb. The original tomb was broken to pieces by the Huguenots in the wars of religion of the seventeenth century, but though the stone was broken, the body of the great Duke was not disturbed, for in the year 1822 it was ascertained beyond doubt, on an examination then made, that the skeleton of the Duke still remained untouched, clad in his robes, and his monk's cap on his head, just as he had been laid there in 1086. The tomb, as one now sees it, is—to me, at any rate—a relic of surpassing interest. At the foot this simple (modern) inscription :—

CENOTAPHE DU CTE. GUILLAUME VII.

On a plain brass plate fastened to the stone one reads the following inscription in Latin :—

" Here lies William VII.—Gui Geoffroi, Duke of Aquitaine and of the Picts. Knight, and of this new Monastery the founder. He died in the year 1086. Broken by the insane savagery of the impious, (the tomb) was restored, in the time of Louis XVIII., by the Bishop de Boillé."

There in that simple quiet resting-place, away from all the noise and tumult of the city, rests the great Duke Gui Geoffroi, in his own beautiful Abbey, on the banks of the winding river, by the mills of Chasseignes.

Strolling slowly back into the town, I seemed, in a sort of day-dream, that often fell upon me when walking about alone in Poitiers, to see two people just in front—Philip, King of France, and Gui Geoffroi. It was probably by the road I was then following that they walked back from the Abbey to the Duke's palace on the day that has been spoken of in 1075. King Philip, a young man of twenty-two, talking in an excited tone to the Duke of his troubles with William of Normandy, who had been, he said, the cause of the death of his poor father, King Henry, who had never recovered from the worry that had been occasioned him by the loss of the two great battles he had fought against William in Normandy—at Varaville and Mortemer. "And then," said King Philip, "when he wanted my help—I, who am his lord—against Harold of England, I refused to have anything to do with him. My counsellors warned me—one and all of them warned me—against him from the first. They told me that if I should help him to get together the great booty he was seeking beyond the sea, I should never again have any peace of my life."

> Kar se il li laisse assembler
> La grant richesse d'ultre-mer,
> L'aveir è la grant manantie
> Od la boene Chevalerie,
> Et od l'orguil de Normendie,
> Jamais n'ara paiz en sa vie.
>
> Por ço se deit li Reis pener
> Del Duc Willame destorber,
> K'il ne poisse plus halt munter
> Ne en Engleterre passer.
>
> *Le Roman de Rou*, 11,342.

Which may be rendered into English thus :—

If he (Duke William) were permitted to amass great booty beyond the sea, and possess, as well the great riches (of England), as the good chivalry and the pride of Normandy, never should the King (Philip) have peace of his life. Therefore, the King should put all possible hindrances in the way of Duke William, and not let him rise any higher, or pass over into England at all.

"And see," added King Philip, speaking of William of Normandy, as he walked along side by side with Gui Geoffroi—"see how this man's treating me now. Hasn't he land enough of his own? Think of his trying to rob me of my province of Brittany, and my good fortress of Dol!" And Gui Geoffroi, listening to all this, seemed to speak more gently of his own troubles with Pope Gregory, and suggested that, if the Pope would but give up insisting on his divorce from Aldearden, he would assist him to the utmost of his power in effecting the reforms he was so bent on of the clergy. A little later King Philip was destined to have his own troubles of that sort with the Pope, who excommunicated him on account of his marriage with Bertrade de Montfort, the beautiful but unprincipled Countess of Anjou.

And then, as the conversation I had been—in imagination—listening to ended, the figures of King Philip and Gui Geoffroi disappeared. And looking back from the hillside, as the sun was setting, the flying buttresses of the Abbey, and its exquisitely delicate and beautiful little belfry, stood out hard and clear in the intense red light of the evening sky. It was the very moment to see the Abbey in its greatest beauty—in perfect peace.

The Story of Sainte Radegonde—a Queen of France of the sixth century—the patron saint of Poitiers.

The Story of Sainte Radegonde—a Queen of France of the sixth century—the patron saint of Poitiers.

THE patron saint of the city of Poitiers (jointly with Saint Hilary) is Sainte Radegonde, who was a Queen of France in the sixth century—the wife of Clotaire I., son of Clovis, King of the Franks. She lies buried in the church bearing her name, in the city which, in August every year, is thronged with pilgrims from all parts of France, who there assemble in her honour. It is computed that no less than a hundred thousand pilgrims come to Poitiers in the course of every year to worship at her shrine. The Queen, who was one of the most beautiful and accomplished women of her day, was the daughter of Berthaire, a King of Thuringia—

the country in North Germany that lies between the Weser and the Elbe.

She was born about 520, and while still very young, her father was murdered by his brother Hermenfroy. And upon this—in the year 528—Clotaire, in conjunction with his brother Theodoric, or Thierri, King of Metz, attacked Hermenfroy, beat him, and put him to flight. And, as a result of the war that ensued between them, Thuringia became annexed to Austrasia, a country that then formed the eastern part of France, and Radegonde and her young brother passed as captives into the hands of Clotaire, who had become King of Soissons on the death of Clovis, his brother Clodomir becoming at the same time King of Orleans and Duke of Aquitaine.

At the time of her falling into the hands of Clotaire, Radegonde was a child of exceptional accomplishments and learning, and Clotaire sent her to D'Athies in Vermandois (now known as St. Quentin) to be educated, and secured for her the best possible professors and masters, the most pious and most learned men of the day.

As the result of disputes that soon after the death of Clovis arose between his four sons as to the division of his great kingdom, Clotaire became possessed of Aquitaine and Poitiers, Clodomir having been killed in battle. And on the death of his fourth wife, Queen Consonne, he determined to marry his beautiful captive, Radegonde.

Historians of the time all agree that Radegonde, who was just seventeen years of age, was of surpassing beauty and accomplishments and learning ; but the position of Queen had no attractions for her. On the contrary, as soon as she heard of Clotaire's intention to marry her, she fled away at night, with two of her most trusted companions —Agnès, who was destined afterwards to become Abbess of her great Abbey of Sainte Croix at Poitiers, and her devoted friend and servant—who never left her, and who after her death wrote a story of her life—the nun Baudoyne, Baudonivia, or

Baudonivie—and the three friends hid themselves for
a time in a cave at Nissy-sur-Aisne.   But their flight
availed them little, as they were quickly found by the
messengers sent out by Clotaire in search of them, and
Radegonde was taken by force to Soissons, where
Clotaire married her, and at the same time settled
upon her—according to the custom of the time—as
the "don du matin," property of great value, and large
estates.   Green boughs, freshly cut from the trees on
these estates, were given to the Queen in presence
of witnesses, in token that the King's rights in those
lands were wholly renounced in her favour.   And
thus Radegonde became possessed of ample means
with which to carry out the many great and good
works of charity for which her memory has ever been
and ever will be held in affectionate remembrance
by the people of Poitiers and the country of
Poitou.

Clotaire was, as his brothers were, of a coarse,
fierce, and cruel nature, quite unfitted to be the
husband of a woman as gentle, good, and accom-

plished as the Queen ; but for a short time
Radegonde lived quietly at the Court at Soissons,
devoting herself from the first to acts of charity—
visiting the poor and sick, and especially the lepers,
and helping and comforting the prisoners, while
refusing altogether to accept her position as
Clotaire's wife or to associate herself in any way
with the dissolute and brutal life of her husband's
Court, till suddenly in an access of unreasoning
fury, Clotaire, during her temporary absence in
the country, caused her young brother to be
murdered—that brother who had been her loving
and constant companion all her life, and to
whom she was devotedly attached. And upon
this, the Queen sought out Clotaire, and said
firmly but quietly to him that she intended to
leave him for ever. "The light of my life was my
brother," she said to him. "All the happiness I
ever had in the world has gone with him, and
now I will leave you at once and for ever, and
devote the remainder of my days to the service of

x

God. The days without tears are unknown to me since my brother is gone."

And the King, struck with remorse at the cowardly crime he had committed, gave his consent to the Queen leaving him, and sent an escort of guards with her to Noyon, where she determined to place herself under the care of the Bishop of Noyon — Saint Medard. And on her arrival at Noyon, the Queen proceeded at once to the church where the Bishop (an old man ninety years of age) was performing the office of the mass ; and advancing rapidly towards him, surrounded by her guards, and passing through the midst of the astonished people, clothed in her royal robes, with her diadem and jewels flashing in the sun, she, kneeling down before the high altar, asked for the Bishop's benediction, and that he would give her then and there the habit and order of a nun, and consecrate her at once to the service of the Church. But the Bishop being frightened, drew back : " I am in a marvellous per-plexity," he exclaimed, "and dare not accede to your desire," for he had not heard of the King's consent to what was asked of him. And the soldiers, being frightened at what might come of the step that was being taken, threatened to lay violent hands on the Bishop if he ventured to consecrate or lay hands in any way upon the Queen; and upon this, in the midst of the tumult thus occasioned, the Queen withdrew quickly from the body of the church, and having obtained the black habit of a nun, she threw it hastily over her royal robes, and again appearing in the church and standing at the high altar before the Bishop, she addressed him thus, with eyes flashing with fire, and in a voice that quelled in an instant the tumult of the crowd: "Bishop of God," she exclaimed, "Bishop of God! if you dare to refuse my desire, if fear of men is greater with you than fear of God, remember that one day you shall answer to Him who is the King of Heaven for the sheep that you now refuse to admit into your fold." And upon this, struck by the commanding presence of the Queen, and doubtless (as says the historian Saint Fortunatus) obeying an inspiration from on high, the Bishop, on the instant, gave her the order she besought of him, and consecrated her from that moment to the service of God, the soldiers who had objected now standing by silent witnesses of the scene.

And this done, the Queen deposited on the altar her diadem and jewels, and breaking into small pieces her broad girdle of gold, distributed it to the poor. "I have bidden adieu to the world," she said, "and all its belongings. I have bidden farewell to the world, and I want no more of its ornaments again"

So entered Queen Radegonde into religion; thus thrust she away with scorn her rank and position as Queen of France, and in this manner took she leave for ever of the world.

After a short time, feeling that Noyon was too near the Court to be quite safe for her, the Queen retired first to Tours, then to Candes, where Saint Martin lies buried by the river Loire, between

the Abbey of Fontevraud and Chinon, and at
last to Saix, one of the estates that had been
given her as the "don du matin" on her marriage,
a little town a short distance from Chinon on the
river Vienne, and within the bounds of Poitou, and
there with her friends Agnès and Baudonivie she
determined to pass the preliminary stages of "la
vie religieuse."

And at Saix she remained for a time, wholly
absorbed in the new life she had undertaken, waiting
upon and helping the poor, nursing the sick, and
especially the lepers, without any regard to the
danger of infection, and passing the rest of her time
in meditation and prayer.

At last it entered into the mind of Clotaire that
the Queen should be brought back to the Court, the
splendour of which had been greatly diminished by
her retirement, and he set out with a number of
dissolute companions to take her back—by force if
necessary—to the Court at Soissons; and this gave
rise to one of the miracles, one of many with

which the life of Sainte Radegonde is to this day associated in the minds of the people of the country —"le miracle des avoines" (the miracle of the oats).

When the report reached Saix that the King had determined that Radegonde must go back to the Court, and that he himself was about to set out from Soissons for the purpose of taking her back, a great fear fell upon her, and she sent a trusted messenger, Fridovigia, to John of Chinon, a hermit, living in a cave near Chinon, with jewels of great value, entreating him that he would pray to heaven for her that she should not be compelled to return into the world. And the hermit, after much prayer, sent the Queen a message that the King's desire to take her back to the Court was all very well. She need, he said, in no way dispute it; she need make no opposition, no objection, but let things take their course, resting perfectly assured that heaven would not permit any such thing as Clotaire intended to be done.

And Clotaire proceeded on his journey to Saix.
And on hearing in the courtyard of her house the
footsteps of the horses that announced the arrival
of his party, the Queen and her attendants, Agnès
and Baudonivie, fled quickly away into the fields.
And there they met a peasant who at the moment
was sowing a crop of oats. And the Queen
approaching him said, "My friend, I wish you
good morning. If anyone should pass by and ask
you, 'Have you seen the Queen pass this way?
Which way has gone the Queen?' say to them,
'No person has passed this way since I sowed this
crop of oats.'" And upon this the oats sprang up
into ear immediately, and the Queen and her companions could nowhere be seen, for in a few
moments the ears of the oats were waving over their
heads—the Queen's, and Agnès's, and Baudonivie's.
And Clotaire coming to the spot shortly afterwards,
and being told by the peasant of what had happened,
and witnessing with astonishment that miracle,
acknowledged the divine intervention, and returned

straightway to his Court at Soissons and troubled the Queen no more.

Thus was miraculously fulfilled the prediction of John the Hermit of Chinon, and to this day the tradition of the miracle is devoutly believed in by the people of the country. A special fête and a special service is held in commemoration of the miracle every year in Poitiers by the nuns of Sainte Croix.

Shortly after this Queen Radegonde, whose residence at Saix was but a step preparatory to the final life of the cloister, came to Poitiers for the purpose of building and establishing there the famous Abbey of Sainte Croix. And in this she had not only the warm approval and support of Clotaire and his sons, but they assisted largely in paying the cost of the building and in providing its endowment. The Abbey was built just within the Roman walls of the city, the walls and towers forming part of the cloisters on the eastern side.

And at about the same time the Queen—the King and his sons supporting her — commenced building the Church of Sainte Radegonde, which was placed near the Abbey, but just outside the city walls, as the Queen desired that she and the nuns of Sainte Croix should be buried in the church when completed, since by the Roman law burial in the Abbey, which was within the walls of the city, was not allowed. At first the church was dedicated to Our Lady the Virgin; after the Queen's death it was re-dedicated to her.

In the crypt of the existing church (a crypt of sixth century construction) the Queen lies buried, and the nuns near her. The original church was burnt in a great fire at the end of the eleventh century, and was reconstructed at, or shortly after, that date, as one sees it now. The fine massive sarcophagus in the crypt is believed to be the original sarcophagus in which Gregory of Tours, her intimate friend, himself deposited the body of the Queen.

The beautiful tower at the west entrance to the

bench for the prisoners and their advocates. The side walls of all these enclosures are decorated at each corner with crouching lions in stone, at this distance of time almost worn away, but still distinguishable. It is believed that from lions such as these the ancient ecclesiastical jurisdiction—" Inter leones "—took its name.

A somewhat similar jurisdiction, founded by the Moors, is, I believe, still in force in some parts of Spain, where a tribunal known as the " Tribunal of the Waters," with judges and attendants clothed in picturesque costumes of the Middle Ages, administers rude and summary justice to the people of the country at the entrance door or porch of the Cathedral of Valentia once every week, and there may not improbably be similar tribunals in other parts of Spain.

On the 25th October, A.D. 552, the Abbey of Sainte Croix was completed, and on the arrival of Saint Germain, the Bishop of Paris, who was appointed to represent the King at the opening ceremony, the

Queen, escorted by two hundred nuns, clothed in black—all of them ladies of noble birth, some of them the daughters of kings—walked, in a great and splendid procession, through the streets of the city, amidst the acclamations of the people, who in a dense throng crowded even the housetops ; and so they passed within the walls of the Abbey, and the life of the cloister was begun.· A little later, the Queen's friend, Agnès, a simple nun, was elected Abbess, and shortly after this King Clotaire died—"Il alla de vie à trespas," says the old chronicle—at Compiegne, of a fever caught when hunting stags in the forest. He was then at the height of his power, in the fifty-first year of his reign—King of all France and the dominions of Clovis. Clotaire is said to have heartily repented of his many sins before he died, and it is recorded of him that almost his last words were—"Elva ! Elva ! quam magnus est Rex ille cælestis qui sic humiliat sublimes terræ Reges !"—that is, " He is indeed great, the King of Heaven, who thus brings low the greatest of the earth. And as He is immortal, so is He better than kings and princes, and all the dwellers on the earth, who die and pass away. And as He is better, so is He more powerful. And as He is more powerful, so is He the giver of grace and pity to us all. He takes no pleasure, as men do, in the destruction of the wicked, but is sweet and debonnaire, and He has compassion upon the penitence of sinners who return to Him. It is His wisdom that inspires with hope the hearts of all of us, and none need despair of the infinite goodness of His mercy." With these words upon his lips, and commending the Queen and her Abbey of Sainte Croix to the care and protection of his sons, the great King passed silently and peacefully away. He died on the 10th November, A.D. 561, and lies buried in his city of Soissons, in the church of Saint Medard. He is said to have been the first King of France who made coins of gold—"fait battre de la monnoie d'or," which the Emperor Justinian decreed should be used in commerce throughout the Empire, provided his own image was stamped upon them.

At Clotaire's death, Caribert, one of his sons, became King of Aquitaine and Poitou, and ruler of Poitiers.

In the year 569 the Emperor Justin II. (the successor of Justinian) sent as a present to the Queen one of the most precious relics that was ever received in the city of Poitiers in days when such things were regarded as of inestimable value —a large piece of the true Cross, magnificently enshrined, which was brought from Constantinople to Poitiers by the hands of Saint Euphronius, the then Bishop of Tours. By order of Sigibert, son of Clotaire and King of Eastern France, Saint Euphronius, after he had reached Tours with the relic, set out with it for Poitiers surrounded by the clergy and a great concourse of attendants and the principal people of the country, carrying lighted torches, and headed by choristers, who never ceased to sing the hymns of the Church during the whole of the journey, as, by the special order of the King, they walked in procession on foot, a distance of about sixty miles, through the beautiful country of Poitou and Touraine.

And at the distance of about a league from the city of Poitiers they were met by the delegates of the Queen and the great lords of the country and all the principal inhabitants of the city. And here the procession was re-formed, and by a great and splendid company the sacred relic, the present of the Emperor, was taken to the abbey, the flags and banners of Aquitaine waving everywhere in the air, and the choristers singing as a song of triumph, as the procession passed through the streets, the Latin hymn, "Vexilla Regis," that had been specially composed for the occasion, and given to the Queen. The "Vexilla Regis" is a Latin hymn composed by Venantius Fortunatus, a student of Ravenna, a fine poet and historian, a man of noble birth and of the highest taste and cultivation, and one of the most distinguished scholars of his day; he left his country and his home in Italy to go to Tours in early life, we are told, for the "love of Saint Martin," and from

Electa digno stipite
Tam sancta membra tangere.

VI.

Beata, cujus brachiis,
Pretium pependit sæculi,
Statera facta est corporis
Prædam tulitque Tartari.

VII.

Fundis aroma cortice,
Vincis sapore nectare,
Jucunda fructu fertili
Plaudis triumpho nobili.

VIII.

Salve ara, salve victima
De passionis gloria
Qua vita mortem pertulit
Et morte vitam reddidit.

I have rendered the words into English, thus :—

I.

Sweep on, the banners of the King.

In heaven the mystic Cross we see.

The Maker of our flesh, in flesh,

On high is hung upon the tree.

II.

The fastened nail—the suffering form—

The outstretched hands that stain the wood,

Here as a sacrifice He stands,

So doth He bring us back to God.

III.

On high upon the Cross He's bound,

And from His wounded side the flood

Doth wash and cleanse us of our sins,

In stream of water mixed with blood.

IV.

Now is fulfilled what David sang
 In song triumphant, song divine :
God is the King of earth and heaven,
 And from the Cross His love doth shine.

V.

Oh, tree most beauteous ! tree most fair !
 Adorned with purple of the King ;
The worthiest tree in all the wood,
 Doth this last tender service bring.

VI.

Oh, happy tree ! upon whose arms
 The ransom of the world was shown,
By Him we're snatched from Satan's power,
 Who doth by death for sin atone.

VII.

Thrice happy tree ! thy bark distils
 Sweet scent of cedar through the air,

Happy in thine abundant fruit,

Thou in this triumph hast thy share.

VIII.

All hail! all hail, most glorious King!

Thy passion saves us, suffering Lord ;

Our life, no more than death did bring,

Yet by Thy death is life restored.

Here again, as in the " Pange lingua," the opening
verse of the hymn contains a reference to the
standard—the " Labarum " that stood in front of the
Emperor Constantine's statue by the church of
St. Nicholas in Poitiers, now known as Notre-Dame-
la-Grande.

A very interesting story of the life and miracles
of Sainte Radegonde was written—at the request
of the nuns of Sainte Croix—by one of their order,
the nun Baudonivie. The prologue to the story—
which I have translated from the sixth century Latin
—is so exceedingly poetical, touching, and picturesque

that it is here quoted almost in its entirety, both
for the qualities that have been mentioned and for
its beauty of style :—

"To the holy women adorned with the grace of
goodness, to the Abbess Didimia and the whole
assembly of the nuns of the glorious lady, Queen
Radegonde, Baudonivie, the lowliest of your order,
thus speaks to you. In writing the life of the
blessed Sainte Radegonde, who is so well known to
us all, and of whom all of us can say something,
you have put upon me a work the right performance
of which is not less impossible to me than it would
be to touch the heavens with my fingers, for such
a task should be entrusted to those who have the
gift of eloquence, whence what is assigned to them
may be the more beautifully told in a soft flowing
song. But some who are of great learning have
not the gift of eloquence, and these, though they
may desire to write well what is asked of them, are
timid. As for myself, I know very well that I am
but a person of little importance, having small

power of eloquence or understanding, and I feel in a
difficulty that what may be said to the learned may
to the unlearned be just as well left unsaid, for the
one class are accustomed to discern great things in
little, the other knows not how to place little things
in comparison with great, so that what by some is
thought much of, by others is distrusted or lightly
esteemed. When therefore I, who am the least of all
the little ones, submit myself in obedience to your most
precious will, I pray that I may be assisted by you
with the power of speech; little learning have I,
but I am the more earnest. And not those things
will I repeat that the Apostle Fortunatus, the
Bishop, has already written concerning the life of
the Saint, but those things only that in the greatness
of the subject he has passed over without notice—
things that in his book he referred to when, speaking
of the many qualities of the Saint, he said: ' Let
brevity suffice for my purpose, and let not the great
wealth of the subject be lightly thought of in a case
where by a few instances only such complete know-

ledge may be obtained.' Therefore, the divine power inspiring me, and He whom the blessed Saint ever sought to please and follow while with us here on earth, and with whom she now reigns in heaven in glory—not in fine language, but in homely words, will I endeavour in this discourse to speak out to you all of the many miracles of the Saint of which but few have yet been told."

An account is given in Baudonivie's story of many miracles not recorded by Saint Fortunatus or by Gregory of Tours (who both wrote lives of the Queen), and one of the most remarkable and striking of these has reference to the miraculous deliverance from shipwreck of certain messengers of the Queen. The story is thus told by Baudonivie: "After the sacred relic of the true cross had been deposited in the Abbey of Sainte Croix, the Queen sent certain of her servants and other trusted messengers to Constantinople to return thanks to the Emperor in person for his present, and as they returned a great storm arose upon the sea, and for forty days and forty nights the ship was tossed upon the waters, and the messengers, making their peace with heaven, gave themselves up for lost. At last, despairing of all hope of life, they prayed thus to Radegonde: 'Lady Radegonde! (Domina Radegonde) help thy servants, that in carrying out thy commands we perish not in the depths of the sea. Deliver us, we pray thee, out of the hands of death, for the sea is ready to destroy us. Have pity on us thy servants, who are in great misery. Help us or we die.'"

And to the sound of the voices there came through the air a dove in the midst of the storm, and circling three times round the ship, at the third turn, in token of the Trinity, which, says Baudonivie, the blessed Saint had ever in her mind, a servant of the Queen, by name Banisaius, extended his hand to the bird as it flew by, and from its tail he drew three feathers, with which, touching the sea, he moderated the storm. And upon hearing those sailors call upon the name of the saint, the dove that had appeared rescued them from the jaws of death, for immediately a great stillness fell upon the waters and the sea was calm. And the men with one voice exclaimed, "Good Lady, by thy great holiness, from the peril of the sea thus hast thou snatched us from death, and from the midst of the waters." And the men who were thus saved deposited those feathers of the dove and many other offerings of their own as relics in the churches in the city of Poitiers.

In the year 570 the Queen and the Abbess Agnès went together to Provence to study, on the spot, the rules of the order of Saint Cæsar of Arles, and after careful examination of the rules they adopted them, without any alteration, for the Abbey of Sainte Croix.

It is related by Baudonivie that a year before her death the Queen had a vision that she had ascended into heaven, to the place allotted to her in Paradise, and that Christ had appeared to her and spoken to her as she was praying in her church

Pl. XXIV

which, according to the belief of that time, Christ was born.

The story of her death is most pathetically and beautifully told by Baudonivie, who was present, and by an old French writer, Dumonteil.

Down to the day of her death the Queen allowed of no interruption whatever of her work. On a Wednesday, as she had foreseen—on the morning " de la quatrième férié "—that is the fourth of the August days that are now celebrated as her annual festival at Poitiers—on the 13th of August, 587, the Queen passed quietly away in the midst of the nuns assembled round her in the deepest tribulation, praying intently and with one voice that she might be spared to them. "And at that moment," says Baudonivie, "some stonemasons, servants of the Queen, who were hewing stone in the quarry on the opposite hill, heard in the air the voice of an angel, speaking as if to other angels, who were invisible, 'What are you doing ? Leave her there upon the earth; let her rest where she is, for the prayers of the nuns have ascended to heaven, and the Queen's life is to be spared.'—'It is too late,' said the answering voices—'It is too late,' said the angels who were bearing her soul away; 'it is too late, for the Queen hath already entered into Paradise; she hath already entered into the joy of her Lord.'"

"We thought," adds Baudonivie, "that we should not be separated from her—we who are the faithful servants of Him with whom in heaven she reigns. And now it remains to us not so much to bewail her loss, as in fear and trembling to look forward, for we have indeed sent before us a lady and a mother, who will ever be an intercessor for us in heaven, in the kingdom of God; a friend who hath left to us a sorrow that is greater than we can bear, but in the heavens will obtain for us a glory that is eternal and a peace that passeth not away."

Such was the vision of the stonemasons at the passing away of the Queen—a touching and beautiful tradition—devoutly believed in, to this day, by the people of the country and the nuns of Sainte Croix.

The above is, of course, but a short and imperfect account of the life of Sainte Radegonde ; for a complete account reference should be made to the works of Gregory of Tours, Fortunatus, and Baudonivie. A beautiful eulogy has been written of the Queen, and a history of her life, by her friend Gregory, Archbishop of Tours, the father, as he has been called, of the history of France. A story of her life has also been written by her intimate friend and fellow-labourer, Saint Fortunatus, sometime Bishop of Poitiers.

Of the estimation in which the memory of the Queen is still held in Poitou, one may judge somewhat from the fact of the pilgrimages that have been referred to. There is hardly a print-seller's or bookseller's shop in the city of Poitiers that does not contain her likeness in some form— print, photograph, or model. Her memory still, after more than fourteen hundred years, remains

supreme in the affections of the people of the
country, and above all is revered and treasured
as none other is by the simple-minded country
people, the poor people she did so much for, the
peasants of Poitou.

The Story of the building of the new City of Poitiers, about A.D. *46. And of the Cathedral of Saint Pierre. And of the earlier Christian Church that once stood upon the site occupied by the cathedral in the days of Saint Martial, the Apostle of Aquitaine.*

ON the eastern slope of the steep hill on which the city of Poitiers is built, about midway between the two main streets—the Rue du Pont Neuf and the Grande Rue—that run in parallel lines down to the river Clain, at a short distance only from the foot of the hill, stands the Cathedral of Poitiers—Saint Pierre.

The cathedral is a twelfth century building, the first stone of which was laid by Queen Eleanor, Duchess of Aquitaine and Countess of Poitiers, wife of King Henry II. of England, in the year 1162. About two hundred and seventeen years were occupied in its construction. The Queen's

Still not a word of reply was returned to anything I said! At last, with a momentary air of thought and an expression of great benignity, he said to me: "Monsieur is mistaken; Thomàs never was here!" Then it occurred to me that to have spoken of the Saint as Becket, and not as Thomàs, was a most unfortunate mistake.

"Thomàs," he repeated slowly, but very emphatically, as if he entertained not a shadow of a doubt on the subject, "Thomàs never was here!" And the sacristan coming up at the moment, he said to him, "Show this gentleman all that he desires to see; show him the blue crozier, and the pictures, the pictures of the bishops, and the crypt, and the windows—all that there is to be seen." And, with a polite bow to me, he hurried away to his breakfast murmuring, "Thomàs, Thomàs!" and shaking his head as he went. And that was all that I was ever able to learn from the authorities of the history of the Cathedral of Saint Pierre.

To trace out the story of the cathedral, and the

story of the building of the city of Poitiers, one must go back nearly two thousand years, to that time in the last half of the last century before the birth of Christ, when first the country of Poitou and Gascony with parts of Gaul, and then Britain, were invaded and conquered by the Romans under Julius Cæsar, and subjected to the Roman rule.

Less than a hundred years after the conquest of these countries by the Romans an insurrection broke out in Britain, and the Emperor Claudius, marching with an army through Aquitaine, for the purpose of suppressing it, took with him to England Stephen, the King of Aquitaine, and a certain number of the nobles and picked soldiers of the country of Poitou. And mainly by the assistance of these " Picts," the rebellion was quickly put down. And for this service on their return to their own country the people of Poitou obtained from the Emperor permission to rebuild their city on a new site—that is to say, on the spot where Poitiers now stands. The ancient city, " le vieulx Poictiers," known before the Roman conquest as Limonum, is believed to have occupied a site a good deal to the north of the present city in the direction of the town of Chatellerault.

And this permission the Emperor willingly granted, and about the year A.D. 46 the work of construction was commenced and carried on with great rapidity, and the new city was completed and walled in in the last year of the reign of the Emperor Nero. Much of the Roman work and parts of the ancient walls of the city are still to be seen in various parts of Poitiers.

And whilst the city was being built, Saint Peter, according to an old tradition, sent out his disciples to preach the Gospel throughout the world: Saint Mark was sent to Alexandria, Saint Saturnin to Toulouse, Saint Denis to Paris, and Saint Martial to Poitou and Aquitaine. And from that moment Saint Martial is said to have devoted the remainder of his life to preaching and teaching the Catholic faith in Aquitaine. The town in which he lived and made his home, and where he lies buried, is Limoges, south-east of Poitiers, the ancient capital of the wild and beautiful country of the Limousin.

Saint Martial was, as we are told in the "Legenda Aurea" and other ancient books, the son of a noble Jew named Marcellus, who, when Christ was preaching to the people of Judæa, came to hear Him and was converted, and he and his son were baptised by Saint Peter. And the boy, then about twelve or thirteen years old, remained with Saint Peter, who was so greatly attached to him that they lived always together, till Saint Martial was sent ultimately to Aquitaine.

It is related of Saint Martial by Anthoninus, Archbishop of Florence, that he was nearly related to Saint Stephen ; and that it was he who, as a lad, brought the loaves and fishes to Christ when the people were miraculously fed, as related in the Gospel of St. John. And he is said (in the Golden Legend) to have been the little child whom Christ set in the midst of His disciples when they were disputing which of them should be the greatest. Ordericus Vitalis relates that he was present at the raising of Lazarus, and that he ministered with Cleophas at the Last Supper, and witnessed our Lord's ascension into heaven, after which he remained always with Saint Peter till he left him to go into Aquitaine.

And so it happened that, according to the tradition, Saint Martial was preaching the Gospel to the people of Poitiers on that day, 29th June, A.D. 66, on which Saint Peter and Saint Paul are supposed to have been put to death by the Emperor Nero; and it was in commemoration of that event that the people of Poitiers at once commenced, and shortly afterwards finished, on that spot, a Christian church, upon the foundations of which the great cathedral of St. Pierre now stands. Such, according to this tradition, is the origin of the Cathedral of Saint Pierre, which now replaces the earlier Christian church; and amongst much that is left doubtful about the original building by early writers

this seems to be certain—that about the middle of
the fourth century Saint Hilary, Bishop of Poitiers,
recounted the story of the building of the church (his
own church) to a council of bishops at Rome, and
received from them, in acknowledgment of the
circumstances, in the days when such relics were
of inestimable value, a large portion of the beard
of Saint Peter, which was placed in a magnificently
jewelled shrine, and regarded for many centuries as
one of the most precious treasures of Poitiers.

Bouchet says in the "Annals of Aquitaine" that
it was believed that King Dagobert in the seventh
century removed the famous relic when he was
pillaging the churches of Aquitaine to enrich the
Church of Saint Denis, and that it was then
contained in a casket or *chasse* made of gold and
studded with jewels, among them a sapphire the
size of a walnut. "But for my part," says Bouchet,
"I think it more probable that about the year
1192 Richard Cœur de Lion, King of England
and Count of Poitiers, took the *chasse* and the

jewels, and the croziers and chalices, and all
the gold and silver plate of the churches of Aquitaine to provide the ransom he had to pay to the
Duke of Austria, who seized and imprisoned him on
his way home from the Holy Land, for the relics
were known to have been richly enshrined in the
time of his father and mother, King Henry II. and
Queen Eleanor, and after that they disappeared!"

Saint Martial, having preached the doctrines of
Christianity throughout Aquitaine for a period of
twenty-eight years, fell ill of a fever at Limoges and
died, and his body reposes beneath the Church of
Saint Pierre-du-Sepulchre at Limoges.

The arms of the city of Limoges still contain
the bust of the saint, and the initial letters of his
name, S. M. His name is also connected with the
most ancient bridge of the city, constructed in his
own time by the Romans and named after him,
and with the rich Abbey of Saint Martial and
other buildings in the town.

As the Church of Saint Pierre was built in the

middle of the first century, so it appears to have remained till the time of Louis le Debonnaire, the son of Charlemagne. Towards the middle of the ninth century it was repaired and enlarged, with many other churches and religious houses in Poitiers then requiring reparation, by Louis le Debonnaire, who, after the death of Charlemagne, became King of Aquitaine and Emperor of the West.

After that, in the early part of the eleventh century, A.D. 1018, a great fire consumed part of the city, and with it the cathedral. And at this time Guillaume le Grand was Count of Poitiers and Duke of Aquitaine, the kingdom having some time previously been changed into a duchy, of which the Counts of Poitiers were the ruling princes or dukes. And with great rapidity, for the rebuilding was finished in a little more than three years after the fire, the cathedral was rebuilt with great magnificence by the Duke.

A great and powerful prince was Guillaume le Grand. Treated as an equal by the sovereigns of his time, who were represented by ambassadors at his Court at Poitiers, he was always received by the Pope with the same honours as the Emperor. He was at the same time a great student; a liberal patron of the arts and of men of letters, he sought for and enjoyed the society of the most distinguished scholars of his day. Of fine and cultivated taste, he was the possessor of a famous library, one of the treasures of which was an ancient manuscript in letters of gold, that was sent to him as a present by Canute, King of England, and which is said to have contained valuable proofs of the evangelisation of Poitou by Saint Martial, and of the origin of the city and its Church of Saint Pierre.

The Duke was always an ardent defender of the rights and property of the Church. So great was his position that a few years before his retirement from the world — he retired, as his father Fier-a-bras had done before him, to the Abbey of Maillezais, where he died in 1030 — the great lords

of Lombardy came to him in a body and offered him
the crown of Emperor of the West, an honour he
declined. It was he who, after the fire of 1018,
rebuilt the ancient palace of the Dukes of Aquitaine
in Poitiers, now known as the Palais de Justice. It
was his son Gui Geoffroi who, after another disastrous
fire at the end of the eleventh century, rebuilt the
palace with the magnificent hall, the "Salle du
Palais," or "Salle des Gardes," now known as the
Salles des Pas-perdus. The remainder of the ducal
palace, as we now see it, the three magnificent fire-
places side by side, the very beautiful windows and
gallery over them, the striking Tour de Maubergeon,
and the other towers, much best seen from the Rue
des Cordeliers, are of late fourteenth century construction, built by Jean de Berri, Count of Poitiers,
after another disastrous fire, said to have been
caused by the English about the year 1365.

In January, 1079, in the time of Gui Geoffroi, son
of Guillaume le Grand, the cathedral was the scene of
a great assembly or synod of bishops, called together

2 D

there by order of Pope Gregory VII., to make severe
rules for the reformation of the clergy, and in particular
to address a threat of excommunication to the French
King, Philip, for his scandalous behaviour, and acts of
oppression and simony towards the Church.   Hugues
de Dié, the Pope's legate, was appointed to preside
over the assembly, and on the 15th January, 1079,
attended by the bishops, robed and with their mitres,
in great state, he entered the cathedral, and the
King's trial, so to speak, was begun.   Upon this,
while the bishops were debating the matter, two of
their own order—friends of the King—the Archbishop of Tours and the Bishop of Rennes, prelates,
we are told, "simoniacal and rebellious," burst into
the building at the head of a body of armed men, and
in a hand-to-hand fight with the Pope's messengers,
some of whom were severely wounded, dispersed the
assembly by force.

A few months later, in October, 1079, the cathedral was the scene of a great public rejoicing of the
people of Poitou and Aquitaine, when Gui Geoffroi,

after a short but very brilliant campaign with the Count of Toulouse, the friend and companion of Godfrey of Boulogne—he who is so well known to us all as Raymond of Saint Gilles, Count of Toulouse, one of the heroes of the first crusade—returned in triumph to his capital, and a great public thanksgiving for this victory was offered in the cathedral.

It would be wearisome to tell of all of them, but many and great must have been the historical scenes that the Church of Saint Pierre witnessed throughout the tenth, eleventh and twelfth centuries, the days of the greatest power, the times most famous in the annals of Aquitaine—the tenth century days, when Louis d'Outremer, King of France, restored the Duchy of Aquitaine and its ancient capital of Poitiers to the fair-haired William Tête-d'Étoupes, he who married Heloïse of Normandy—the daughter of William Longuespée, son of Rollo the Pirate, the first Norman Duke—the story of whose courtship and wedding is so delightfully told us in the Romance of Rollo, the Anglo-Norman " Roman de Rou," and the days of his son, William Fier-a-bras, he of the iron strength, and of his son, the greatest of the race, whom we have already spoken much of, Guillaume le Grand, and his son, Gui Geoffroi, and his son, William, Count of Poitiers, the world-famous Provençal poet, crusader and troubadour, and his son, the hermit Prince William, as the old books say, "now a saint in Paradise," the father of Alienor, or Eleanor, of Aquitaine, the English Queen.

This famous church, the cathedral of the city, must of necessity have been closely connected with all the stirring historical events of those three hundred years, when Aquitaine was a country richer and more important than all the rest of France together, its rulers princes of greater power and greater influence than kings—from the time of Tête-d'Étoupes, who fought and defeated Lothaire, the French King (who had presumed to give Aquitaine, as a fief of France, to his son, Hugh Capet), to the time of William the Hermit Prince, father of our Queen Eleanor, ancestor of the long line, that since the time of Queen Eleanor has remained unbroken, of all our English Kings and Queens.

Volumes might be filled with the stories that could be told of the city and its cathedral in the course of those three hundred years. But for these in these short tales of Aquitaine there is no space. Two or three only—two or three of the last —will leave us nearly at that date at which was commenced—in 1162—the present cathedral, the building that now rests upon the foundations of the church built in the time of Saint Martial, and on those of the larger, and finer, and later buildings of Louis le Debonnaire and Guillaume le Grand.

In the month of November, A.D. 1100, the cathedral was the scene of an event of great historical importance, when the legates of the Pope, and an assembly of bishops and abbés of the Church to the number of one hundred and forty, met there, and pronounced an unanimous sentence of excommunication against Philip, King of France, for his many offences against the Church, and in particular for having

refused to abandon all further relations with Bertrade
de Montfort, the beautiful Countess of Anjou.

William, Count of Poitiers and Duke of Aquitaine,
son of Gui Geoffroi, was present at this conference,
and on the bishops subsequently proceeding to take
into consideration, as they had been directed by the
Pope to do, the question of the validity of his own
marriage with Philippa, the great heiress of Toulouse,
he retired from the cathedral in a state of uncon-
trollable fury, with a large body of his friends,
threatening the bishops with violence as he passed
through the midst of them and left the building, and
immediately afterwards he had the assembly dispersed
and driven in all directions by showers of stones.
And soon after this, in the following spring, he left
the country for a time, to fight the battles of the
Church in his famous but most disastrous crusade in
the Holy Land.

In 1106 the bishops were again called together
in the cathedral, under the guidance of the Papal
legate Bruno and the famous crusader Bohemond,

Prince of Antioch, for the purpose of promoting a further crusade, and a large number of the citizens of Poitiers and the people of the country were induced to leave their homes and go to the assistance of their distressed and unfortunate brethren in the Holy Land.

And shortly after this the cathedral was the scene of a very remarkable and most interesting contest between Duke William, who had now returned from Palestine, and the old Bishop of Poitiers—Bishop Pierre.

In those days, and long afterwards, sentence of excommunication was the strongest weapon of the Church in the assertion of its authority, and was made use of continually without mercy, and without scruple. And so it happened that, on account of some private scandal, which, according to the later authorities—authorities of the highest repute, viz., Vaissette, and the Benedictine monks, the authors of " L'Art de Verifier les Dates des Faits Histo-riques "—would seem to have had no foundation in

fact, Duke William was threatened with excommunication by the Bishop of his own city—Poitiers.

The Duke treated the threat with contempt, but
being one day in attendance at the cathedral at the
service of the Mass, the Bishop suddenly began to
read out against him a sentence of excommunication ;
upon which, in a state of fury, he advanced with
drawn sword towards the Bishop, and, standing immediately in front of him, threatened him with instant
death unless he desisted from the continuation of
that sentence and gave him absolution at once.
The Bishop paused as if frightened, then, gathering
himself together with a great effort, he hurled the
few remaining words of the dread sentence at the
Duke, and calmly said to him, "I have done my
duty—now strike !"

And the Duke, repenting of his threat, quietly put
up his sword, and replied, "I love you not enough
to send your soul to Paradise, but I shall send your
body into exile for evermore." And Pierre was
deprived of his See, and expelled forthwith to the

neighbouring town of Chauvigny, where he died in exile in 1115.

Twelve years after this the Duke passed away—"alla de vie à trespas"—in the year 1127. He had reigned in his capital of Poitiers over the great country of Aquitaine and Toulouse for more than forty years. Poet, crusader, troubadour, the first poet of Provence, and one of the most famous, the first builder up of the beautiful language, the "lingua aulica," as Dante called the language of the court as distinguished from that of the common people, he lies buried with his father, Gui Geoffroi, in the Benedictine Abbey of Montierneuf in the city of Poitiers, on the banks of the beautiful river, by the watermills in the meadows, "les moulins de Chasseignes."

To Duke William succeeded his son William, the Hermit Prince, and father of our Queen Eleanor, wife of Henry II. And during his time there occurred in the cathedral (the authors of " L'Art de Verifier les Dates " say " dans une eglise de Poitiers," but it was probably the cathedral) one of the most

2 E

remarkable scenes that can ever have been witnessed
in any church—that famous scene between the Duke of
Aquitaine and Saint Bernard that is related in many
ancient chronicles, and is, perhaps, one of the most
important historical events of the time.   On the
14th February, 1130, the Pope Honorius died at
Rome, and during the night of his death, and before
the fact became generally known, certain of the
cardinals, sixteen in number, knowing that there
would be a contest in the election of his successor,
met secretly and elected Innocent II. as Pope.   On
the next morning Pierre de Léon (who assumed the
name of Anacletus) was elected Pope by twenty-one
other cardinals.   Saint Bernard, the famous Abbot
of Clairvaux, who was then fast rising to the height
of his power, took the side of Innocent.   And
France and the western states following Saint
Bernard, acknowledged Innocent, and denounced
Anacletus as the anti-Pope.   But in the contest that
ensued in Italy the party of Anacletus prevailed,
and Innocent was driven out of the country

and took refuge at Avignon in France. One prelate alone in the whole of France—Gerard, Bishop of Angoulême—seems to have supported the cause of Anacletus, and being a great personal friend of Duke William, he prevailed upon the Duke to expel from his dominions the bishops and clergy who acknowledged the authority of Innocent, and to replace them by friends of his own ; and so the Bishop of Poitiers was driven into exile, and clergy who could be relied on to support the authority of Anacletus were established in Poitiers and throughout the country of Aquitaine. Upon this the bishops of all the provinces of Southern France assembled themselves at Puy, unanimously recognised the authority of Pope Innocent, and, as a first step in the contest that this produced, passed a sentence of excommunication both against Anacletus and the Duke, and for three or four years the South of France was given over to all the turmoil, misery and scandal of a bitter religious war.

At last Saint Bernard intervened, and in the year 1135, deputed by Innocent, he came to Poitou, accompanied by Geoffrey, Bishop of Chartres, to reason with the Duke, who met them by appointment at Parthenay, a town at no great distance west of Poitiers.

Here Saint Bernard and the Bishop of Chartres did their utmost to persuade the Duke by gentle words to renounce the cause of Anacletus and restore the banished clergy to their dioceses, and warned him of the fate of Dathan and Abiram, whom the earth swallowed up alive for the sin of schism. They insisted on the unity of the Church, and urged that the country of Aquitaine alone in the whole of France stood opposed to the Pope's authority. And to all their arguments the Duke listened with much attention, and then replied very quietly that it mattered nothing in the world to him which of the rival Popes was the true Pope. He cared nothing about it. They might have any Pope that pleased them. He would acknowledge Innocent if they liked, and renounce Anacletus, but as to the bishops and clergy whom he had expelled from his country, those men were detestable to him and nothing should induce him to restore them, or to have anything to do with them again.

A few days after this, Saint Bernard and the Bishop of Chartres went together from Parthenay to Poitiers, and the cathedral of Saint Pierre. The occasion was a great one, the church was crowded with the people of the city, Saint Bernard himself performed the office of the Mass, and the people, trembling and excited at the appearance of the famous preacher, waited as if in expectation of some miracle from heaven, for the report had gone far and wide through the city that some terrible scene between the Duke and Saint Bernard would almost certainly occur. And whilst the excitement was at its height, Saint Bernard, amidst breathless silence, performed the stupendous miracle—as men then thought it—of consecrating the elements. Then rising up suddenly in an ecstasy of enthusiasm, with eyes flashing, and countenance of fire, and a voice trembling with excitement and emotion, he passed quickly through the terrified people, and approached the Duke, who, being an excommunicated person, stood with his courtiers just outside the door of the cathedral—enter it he dared not—and holding the host on high— with outstretched hands above his head, in loud tones of menace and anger he addressed him thus: "We have besought you," he said, "with gentle words, and us, God's ministers, you have despised. A great assembly of the servants of God has entreated you, and with contempt you have rejected their prayer. Behold! the Son of God now approaches you, the Lord and Head of that Church you have despised and injured. Your Judge is now before you, at whose name every knee that is in heaven and earth must bow. Your Judge is present, into whose hands your soul must fall. Will you despise Him? Will you treat Him as you have treated us, His servants?" And high above his head Saint Bernard held the host, and paused for the Duke's reply.

And a silence as of death reigned over the people, and the Duke, paralysed with terror, sank in a fit to the ground. His courtiers and attendants raised him after a few moments, but his terror was so great at the awful scene that had passed before him, that he could neither speak nor see, and, again foaming at the mouth, he sunk senseless on the ground.

And after a short pause Saint Bernard again approached him, and pushing, with a gesture of contempt, his prostrate body with his foot, commanded him to stand up and listen to the judgment of God. "Here is the Bishop of Poitiers," said Saint Bernard, "whom you drove from his church; be reconciled to him with the kiss of peace. Lead him back to his See, whence you wrongfully expelled him; and give glory to God instead of contumely; and restore henceforth throughout your dominions that unity of which, through you, it has been deprived." And the Duke, who neither dared, nor indeed was able, to speak, received the Bishop with the kiss of peace, and restored him to his diocese, and reinstated the expelled clergy; and thus happily ended the great schism in Aquitaine.

Not long after this—in July, 1137—the Duke's daughter Eleanor, heiress to all his princely fortune and estates, married Louis VII., King of France and afterwards (1152), on their divorce by the Council of Beaugency on the ground of near relationship or parenté, she married Henry II., King of England. And in the year 1162, after the destruction of the older church by fire, the first stone of the new cathedral of Saint Pierre—the existing church — was laid by King Henry and Queen Eleanor as Duke and Duchess of Aquitaine. The building was not completely finished and consecrated till October, 1379. Many a story hangs no doubt to the new building; many events of great historic interest must have happened in it during the long wars that were carried on between France and England in the twelfth, thirteenth, fourteenth, and fifteenth centuries for the recovery of the French provinces that became annexed to the crown of England on the marriage of Henry II. and Queen Eleanor ; but it may well be that none of them are of greater interest than those earlier stories, some few of which have been collected together in these Annals of Aquitaine.

FINIS.

LONDON:
PRINTED BY WILLIAM CLOWES AND SONS, Limited,
STAMFORD STREET AND CHARING CROSS.

CPSIA information can be obtained at www.ICGtesting.com
Printed in the USA
BVOW09s1411080216

435949BV00018B/201/P